Country Flavor

Country Flavor

BY

HAYDN S. Sanborn PEARSON

Whittlesey House

MC GRAW-HILL BOOK COMPANY, INC.

New York   London

*This book is produced in full compliance
with the government's regulations for con-
serving paper and other essential materials.*

First Printing

PUBLISHED BY WHITTLESEY HOUSE
A division of the McGraw-Hill Book Company, Inc.

Printed in the United States of America

Contents

YOU'LL LIKE THIS BOOK OF FARM AND RURAL LIFE ESSAYS. COMING at a time when all of us are pretty much weighed down with the burdens of world conflict and perplexed at the vast and uncertain scope of things to come, you'll find "Country Flavor" especially welcome and appropriate. Not because it gives you a chance to forget today's troubles by harking back to the simple life of yesterday, but because it portrays, in vivid word pictures, the good lessons that can be learned from the habits and traditions of life on the farm only a generation ago.

Mr. Pearson knows whereof he speaks. He was born in the New Hampshire hills 44 years ago, where his father, a country minister, owned and ran a 120-acre general farm with a dozen milk cows and an 800-tree orchard. He gained his early education in a one-room school and in the pursuit of the usual chores that are the lot of every farm boy. After he graduated from the University of New Hampshire, and since that time, he has been writing, lecturing and teaching school, all the while, however, staying close to the soil on his own small farm in eastern Massachusetts. He therefore properly qualifies as a countryman.

It is in just that capacity that Mr. Pearson writes his lovely, inspirational pieces on country life that have been appearing in the editorial columns of the *New York Times* now for a number of years, and it is from that full batch that the 75 essays within these covers have been chosen as worthy of a permanent place on the bookshelf. Little quarrel can be had with this selection by the editors and certainly none with the arrangement, which takes the reader from the first stirrings of Spring on the farm in February right through the whole year's strenuous work down to the following January and the ice harvest. The beautiful photographs of country scenes and farm activities are a worthy complement to the text.

Life regards Mr. Pearson's essays as "among the most delightful bits of nature writing now being done in the United States"; nor can their universal appeal be denied. The country boy, now a successful business man in the city, will certainly enjoy reminiscing over his early days of picking stones and mending fences, of shelling corn and hauling out the wood. The country boy who has remained on the farm will like to recall those same days, and then contrast them with present-day methods of scientific farming, perhaps in some respects with misgivings. As for the born and bred urbanite, I venture the guess that some of Mr. Pearson's sketches will literally pull him out of his city box on a shelf (otherwise called an apartment), in search of "that place in the country" without any further delay.

It's not easy to sing Mr. Pearson's praises softly. Aside from his facility of expression, he has an ability to draw a picture that fairly comes to life right before your eyes. "Watering Troughs" and "Bells in Winter" are two good examples. Just as enjoyable are the essays on his animal and bird friends which one can see he has known intimately and with affection from early youth; although I think that in his "Crow Convention," written with a rare humor, he is just a little unfair to the feathered species. On the other hand, you will have a much higher opinion of "Reddy," the fox, in spite of all his peccadilloes, after you read Mr. Pearson's fair appraisal of him.

If his writing is any indication of interest and adaptability, Mrs. Pearson must find her husband a great help to her in the kitchen. His devotion to the culinary arts is set forth with a special relish and gusto, and many housewives in city and country will appreciate his meticulous directions for making corn chowder and red-flannel hash and beef stew, all à la New Hampshire. The finished products, as he describes them, almost "smell good" right on the printed page.

With equal interest many will read, and perhaps learn, about dowsing rods and democrats, snaths and fellies, and wristers and pungs. All of them spelled work or fun on a New England farm in the early nineteen hundreds.

Here in *The Rural New-Yorker*, we have been friends with Mr. Pearson, and his father before him, for a long time. As the author of our "Countryman's Journal" column, he is a staunch advocate of rural life. He knows its advantages and doesn't want to see them engulfed under a tide of commercialism with its smoky factories and dirty streets, and its shallow, dependent living. I have drawn exactly the same lesson from his "Country Flavor" essays, which, one by one, unfold the story of the perseverance and ingenuity of the men and women who have lived and worked on our farms. The life was hard perhaps, but certainly not without rewards and the satisfaction of a job well done. There is much in this way of living that commends itself to our present generation which right now is so genuinely befuddled.

It has been said that agriculture is the keystone of our national economy. If that is so, and few will deny it, then the reason why we have become so strong and prosperous a nation in so short a span of years, is because our agriculture has been sturdy. And the reason in turn for the strength of this keystone has been the self-reliance preached and practiced by our fathers and mothers. Why then has it become so fashionable, socially and economically, to make light of their solid virtues, particularly when the only alternative offered is a sort of futile living under the "guidance" of world and national planners? Better would it be, it seems, to emulate rather than discard, and to assume responsibility as freely and fearlessly as our parents did. The spirit of the pioneer must be kept alive and strong, and in its quiet, gentle way "Country Flavor" tells you why.

WILLIAM F. BERGHOLD

Editor, *The Rural New-Yorker*
August 15, 1945

SPRING SENDS ITS ADVANCE SCOUTS TO THE SOUTH SIDE of the wood lot. Here the sun's rays seem to concentrate and to warm the late winter air. Inside the woods it is still and frosty, and the accumulated snow crunches squeakily underfoot. But here on the south side of the tree barrier there's a cheerful, brief, preliminary caucus. The snow is moist in front of the windbreak of hemlocks, spruces, and pines. The breeze that infiltrates the conifers is singing a soft aria of the spring that's soon to be.

Just inside the wood is still a mound of dank, pungent sawdust, the calling card of the portable sawmill. Here in the sun one can watch and feel a winter passing. The chickadees are in an old apple tree, singing their husky, alto song. A blue jay flashes across the upland field uttering his rough, defiant scream. Here in the snow, beneath the woods, are the dainty tracks of the wood mouse. Here, also, among the wood's bib of brush and alders, are the tracks of rabbits and foxes. They like to travel along the fringe, where they can see the open field and yet be close to security. Suddenly, from back in the woods, one hears the throbbing drumbeat of the ruffed grouse sending his challenge echoing through the tree aisles.

Down in the valley there's the winding, silver strip of the river, bright in the midday light. Beyond are the blue-green hills of a low mountain range. One hears the far-off bark of a farm dog. Spirals of gray smoke rise from farmhouse chimneys. Here on the south side of the wood lot one hears it—that kindling, warming message that spring is on the way.

F. W. Wentw

Sap's Starting

SUN IS CLIMBING HIGHER. SNOW IS MELTING AT MIDDAY on the south side of the upland pasture. Cumulus clouds move across the blue sky. March wind is whipping the pussy willows and cattails at the edge of the meadow swamps. It's sap time again, and on the farm they are readying for the annual harvest. The buckets are washed; the old, weather-grayed sugar house in the maple grove is set in order.

The grove of gnarled, old, sugar-maple trees is a veteran of many years of intense activity. Contrary to the idyllic bucolicisms of those who have observed but not participated, maple-sugar time is a period of hard work as well as fun. Trees have to be tapped; the sap has to be gathered regularly. Often the snow is still deep in the grove and it's hard work for the horses or the oxen to pull the sled with the big wooden barrel.

When the weather is right, the fire beneath the long evaporator has to be kept going day and night. Today sugaring is a scientific process, and when the thermometer says the density is right, the syrup is ready for the cans. But at least once in the season the family plans a "sugarin' off." Neighbors and friends from town come for the evening. Then there's sugar on snow, a stringy, gooey, sweet, half-warm, half-cold confection—the purest confection of nature. There's warm, whitish sugar, just before it's ready to harden. With doughnuts, hot buttered biscuits, and perhaps a dill pickle or two, it's a feast the gods would not have scorned.

This is part of American folklore, along with barn raisings and quilting bees. The roaring wood fire in the old sugar house, the clouds of steam escaping through cracks in the walls, the lights and shadows, the fun and good neighborliness add up to the fact that it's maple-sugar time again.

S HE IS THE GRACEFUL, GREEN GODDESS OF THE TREE family. One sees her standing in solitary beauty high on the side of a rock-studded, juniper-dotted upland pasture. They are dotted among the oaks, beeches, and maples of the farm woodland. They bend over winding, sand-rutted country roads. There are places where sandy-bottomed, clear-cold brooks sing songs as they ripple over exposed roots.

Men found many uses for the white pines when they began to make a nation in the wilderness. These trees were sacrificed for log cabins and barns, for homes and for mills, for stores and for furniture. The queens among them were marked for the masts of great sailing ships. There are still stands of the trees around northern lakes and along foam-laced rivers, but they are decreasing.

Many there are who love the white pines. They wear a beautiful dress of delicate needles arranged in groups of five. Their slender branches sweep out horizontally with tips that often curve upward. The needles have small but distinct whitish lines on the lower surfaces. The imbricated, brownish cones are things of beauty from the time of formation until the scales obey nature's law and open their hearts that the winged seeds may sail away on currents of air.

The goddess of the trees sings a constant song among her branches. When the breezes are strong, her soft aria is rich and full. There are those who think the pine is plaintive and melancholy; perhaps that is because she prefers gentleness and quietness in a world that's noisy and blatant. As the green-clothed branches sway and move, they seem to be talking among themselves, sometimes almost whispering; again, their conversation is animated and cheerful. Through winter blizzards, spring rains, summer heat, and the frosty starlight of autumn, they live in poise and graciousness. The pines stand calmly and speak gently in a world where men make cacophony and confusion.

Picking Stones

DOUBTLESS MR. WEBSTER DID NOT HAVE THE NORTHEAST in mind when he wrote his definition of a harvest: "The season of gathering grain and fruits; also the gathering of a crop; the product of reward of any exertion." Each spring brings its harvest; the product is the ubiquitous stone pile as a reward of exertion.

Picking stones is a regular spring task on the farm. Many a husbandman feels it is the surest crop of the year, never affected by rain, drought, blizzard, or heat. Come spring, the field that was reasonably clear last season yields a new and abundant harvest. Such is the power of the unlocking of the frozen earth when spring turns the key.

Farmers have developed various techniques for reaping this annual harvest. One school of rural philosophy believes in using a dumpcart and throwing the rocks into it as the horses plod slowly over the ground they recently turned into ribbons of moist brown. Another group considers the efficient tool a stoneboat, so that weight can be transferred on a more nearly horizontal plane. A third band believes the stones should be tossed into piles before they are transferred to a conveyor.

A farm lad, however, has a definite opinion about the whole process. Irrespective of the technique, it is a routine, monotonous job. The recent announcement that a mechanical picker-up of stones will be ready after victory is the best news he has heard regarding conditions on the farm front.

F. W. Went

P ROSE AND POETRY HAVE SUNG PAEANS TO THE GLORY of the covered bridges that reached their heyday a few decades ago and are now almost collectors' items. Sparse has been the praise and little the recognition of the humble plank bridges that span the brooks, creeks, and slough spots of the land. Few are the common, rural architectural links that bind the rock-studded hillsides of New England to the sandy-road, flat stretches of pineland in the South and the creek-traversed, black-soil region of the Midwest.

The unpretentious plank bridge is such a link. It was easy to construct rock-walled embankments opposite each other, lay two sturdy, hardwood logs hewn on one side, and then place two-inch planks of long-lasting oak or maple on the stringers. Sometimes a protective railing was built on each side; more often a log was placed near the ends of the planks.

Men and women who now ride across steel and concrete structures remember the old plank bridges. In the late fall, boys and girls, walking to school, stopped and looked at the skim of ice on the brook, speculating on how long it would be before the village pond would be safe for skating. In winter, one could hang onto the ends of the splintered planks and jump up and down on the ice and enjoy the spine-tingling crackle as it sagged and cracked. In spring, farm boys sat with their legs hanging over the end and fished for the big trout that lived in the shadowy hole beneath.

Plank bridges still serve, on the back roads, away from the ribbons of macadam and concrete that cross-stitch the landscape. The covered bridges are succumbing to the inexorable march of modernity, but there are those who hope that the old plank bridges will span brooks and creeks for a long time to come.

*I*T WAS NOT SO LONG AGO THAT WATER INSTEAD OF GASO-line furnished the liquid needed for motive power. In rural hamlet, country town, and city, the watering trough was a piece of Americana. We are still close enough to the Horse Age for millions of Americans now in cities to look up from their work and see in memory the old watering trough at the edge of the village common.

A typical watering trough was made of oak planks and filled through a cast-iron pipe from the spring on a near-by hillside. Summer and winter, a stream of cold water ran into the trough, the overflow going through a pipe into the ground. The ground in front of the trough, during the warm months, was a muddy pudding—good for a horse's hoofs. In winter, it was frozen into a rough pattern with a necklace of frothy ice around the rim.

Outside, the planks were black and dank, with patches of dark-green moss; inside, slimy smooth with a jungle-thick growth of aquatic plants and, on the bottom, inches of brownish-gray sediment. A small boy, pressing his face into the water on a hot day, imagined he saw the floor of the ocean. What seemed level and fine-grained from above the surface became a mysterious land of serrated valleys, rugged mountains, and volcanic peaks.

About forty years ago, watering troughs went arty. Metal troughs appeared—forerunners of metal horses. These troughs —round, square, or rectangular—still sit beside many a village green. They have fluted pleatwork; imaginative figures protrude here and there; curlicues wind around the rim. It was the rococo era in horse troughs.

There's something solid and reassuring about a civilization when a horse stops at a brimming trough, plunges his head into the clear, cold water, and blows and snorts in unmistakable satisfaction.

Stovepipe Cleaning

*T*HE COUNTRYMAN KNOWS WHEN SPRING HAS ARRIVED. It is always a beautiful day, warm and sunny; the sky's blue counterpane is splotched with masses of cumulus clouds. The bluebirds carol from the apple trees in the back yard; cock pheasants crow from the edge of the mowing, and the farm collie is exploring woodchuck holes along the pasture wall.

This is the day—the day Mother decides to have the stovepipe cleaned. The stovepipe goes from the wood-burning kitchen stove straight toward the ceiling, makes a right-angle turn and runs into the central chimney. From the turn to the spot where it enters the chimney the stovepipe is supported at two-foot intervals by wires. It is practical to have the pipe cross the width of the kitchen. It means comforting heat on cold winter days.

Cleaning the pipe follows a pattern established by experience. Newspapers are optimistically spread over a generous area. Then the pipe is tapped gently at the right-angle turn. However, it is tightly stuck by soot; after a half dozen tentative tugs, the countryman gives a sudden strong pull. The pipe comes apart and a generous quantity of soot is spread over the stove, the wood box, and himself. Next, the upright portion is lifted from the stove connection. Another dose of soot! Halfway across the summer kitchen the pipe is tilted too much and a long trail records the rush to the woodshed door. Finally, every piece is on the ground in the back yard. With a light stick the accumulated soot is tapped out.

Reassembling the pipe should be easy. But stovepipe exists not only to convey smoke; its second major purpose is to test man's patience. After a few lengths have been reassembled, they should maintain their position; but, through some obscure law of physics, the pressures exerted elsewhere keep separating the assembled sections. The task completed, the countryman knows that spring has officially arrived.

T TAKES A DAY OR TWO OF TIME IN A BUSY SEASON OF year, but there's something about mending pasture fences that appeals to a man. The foundation of a pasture fence here in the Northeast is often a stone wall. Built generations ago, the weather-grayed, lichen-etched stones are heaved by frost and undermined by spring rains.

In many instances posts are driven into the ground, leaned against the wall, and wire is strung along the posts. Sometimes gray birches, maple saplings, or young oaks are cut and jammed into the low spots. But, just before time to turn the cows out, the pasture fence must be inspected.

It's pleasant work. There's always the chance of discovering a partridge nest and flushing a mother with her brood of tiny chicks. The wood peewees seem to sing more sweetly on fence-mending day; and the song sparrows, bluebirds, and white throats lift lilting arias. If one is fortunate, he may see a red fox trotting slowly across the rocky upper acres. Down along the edge of the swamp there are flocks of trilliums and the fragile lady's slippers.

Mending pasture fence is a seasonal farm task; but it's one farmers and the boys enjoy. Its functional objective is to get ready for the cows, but perhaps beyond that it's a task that gives a man a chance to get caught up with himself. Urbanites may think it strange, but a farmer can find the world is "too much with him" as surely as can a man working in an upright cave of steel, stone, and cement.

A WEATHER-GRAYED VILLAGE DEPOT IS A DISTANT RELA-
tion of a big-town railroad station; but it has an air
of comfortable, everyday livability that is difficult to find in
a large, hustling, efficient place. A village depot is an adjunct
of measured living, not just a spot from which people go in
a hurry or to which they come in a rush.

It isn't much to look at. The outside is dingy. The inside
is dark. The floor needs sweeping. Slim, the agent, sells
tickets, handles freight, loads the milk cans, and watches
the telegraph. He could improve the light by washing the
windows. But Slim has to pass the time of day, in addition
to his other duties, and passing the time of day requires more
minutes and energy than sophisticated urbanites realize.

A village depot has to be heated; and the tall, big-bellied
stove has to be shaken down and have coal added twice a
day. The villagers who gather in the afternoon to watch the
five thirty-five from the city pull in with the empty milk cans
and an occasional bit of freight wouldn't feel comfortable if
there weren't a generous sprinkling of coal ashes on the
floor.

The depot serves almost as well as the village store for a
community forum. In the morning the farmers exchange
news when they bring the milk cans. A good depot agent
knows as much news as the R.F.D. man and spreads it around
impartially and with judgment. True, trucks and airplanes
are making a difference; but thousands of small towns still
have their depots. If these should disappear, something
would be missing from the rich satisfaction of small-town
life.

Willow Whistle

*T*HE PIPES OF PAN ARE HEARD THESE EARTH-STIRRING days on country roads and rural lanes. A boy and his dog going for the cows are accompanied by a series of shrilly plaintive blasts, for the month of May is willow-whistle season.

There's an art in the construction of the instrument. It requires a craftsman's skill to make the different sizes to produce varied tunes. A country lad knows that the willows along the meadow brook are better than those whose roots find nourishment in higher ground. The juice of life runs richer and more abundantly when the tree roots can reach running water. The bark is tapped loose more easily, and when it dries after the sharp jackknife has made the clean-edge cut for the music-producing area, it clings tighter to the bole as a whistle is jostled in a lad's pocket in intimate juxtaposition with a knife, nails, colored pebbles, marbles, ads cut from the hunting magazines, odd pieces of twine, a few pictures of airplanes, match covers, bottle tops, and a lucky coin.

A boy and a whistle are a sure sign of spring. It's likely to be the tag end, to be sure; but, if the Weather Man insists on hurdling from winter into pre-summer, the willow whistle will at least remind us of the good old days when spring was a recognized season in nature's calendar.

*T*HE ACADEMIC DISCUSSION OVER SETTIN' VERSUS SITTIN' must not be permitted to obfuscate the main issue. One can logically claim that a hen sits; or he can maintain with equal force that he sets her.

A settin' hen has faced obstacles in recent years. Scientific poultry breeders have been striving to eradicate the instinct that induces a biddy to forsake the production of eggs and spend a few weeks cuddling a clutch of eggs and raising a flock of baby chicks. We cannot say how many of the 423,-000,000 hens on 5,150,000 poultry-producing farms will wish to set this spring. We suspect that on many small farms a few clucking mothers will gather their broods beneath their warm feathers.

A settin' hen deserves more serious consideration than the average urbanite may feel inclined to devote to the matter. If given a dozen or fifteen eggs, depending on her over-all sitting capacity, she develops a belligerent but selfless one-track mind. Her consecration to her task is commendable. Often she must be taken from the nest and carried to her daily meal of whole corn and water. Often she must be prevented from reentering the nest until she has eaten and then had a bit of exercise.

Ordinarily hens bask in cheerful human companionship. The countryman claims that hens enjoy his conversation and a verse or two of "Old Black Joe." Hens in the laying pen will talk back and sing to a man—a comforting repartee of mutual admiration. But a hen that wants to set is a different proposition. She prefers solitary confinement, semidarkness and a chance to dream the days away. A little later, when the babies are out, she returns to normal. She may be a fussy, clucking mother, but she's obviously glad to have a human friend about. A settin' hen asks only that while she's settin' she shall have a chance to relax in privacy and get ready for the busy days ahead when she'll have a family to raise.

*T*ECHNICALLY, THE PROCESS OF MILKING A COW IS A method by which the lacteal fluid is extracted. But that is an insufficient explanation to the countryman who likes his cows.

There are those who enjoy milking. When one sits on an old, three-legged stool, close to the smooth, warm flank, with a ten-quart pail between his knees, there's a restful rhythm as the jets of milk shoot downward with steady force. The first few streams play a tune on the metal, and at the end, when the stripping is drawing to a close, the white lines sink into a rounded mass of bubbly froth.

Milking time is restful—provided that bossy has been sprayed to keep the flies away, and that she has a crib full of green oats or the tops of sweet corn on which to munch. As a man automatically pulls the milk, he can philosophize and wonder about the goings on of a topsy-turvy world. A good husbandman treats his cattle so gently that he doesn't have to think about kicking cows or other unruliness. Not that he neglects to part the strands of hair in the tail's brush and tie the tail to the cow's leg. The best of cows will take a swing at a marauding fly, and a tail wrapped forcefully around one's face isn't conducive to pleasant philosophizing.

Milking is far from being the worst job on a farm. In a clean barn, with a fresh layer of pungent sawdust covering the gutters and stanchion floors; with cows chewing noisily and placidly; with two or three cats waiting for supper, while Shep, the collie, watches operations with a guardian eye; a man feels a sense of well-being. We are told that in the marvelous postwar world there will be practical mechanical milkers for all herds; but on many farms there will be men and boys—yes, and women too—who will enjoy drawing the milk from Buttercup and Daisy at the close of day.

F. W. Wentw

WHEN SMALL BANDS OF PIONEERS LEFT THE SETTLE-
ments of Plymouth, Boston, Salem, and Newbury-
port, in the middle 1600's, and pushed to the then distant
lands of southern Maine, southern New Hampshire and the
Connecticut River Valley, they exercised the good judgment
that had brought them to these shores. In most of the new,
tiny towns, the founding fathers set aside an area of "common" land. A "common" meant a place of reasonable security
for the livestock. In the center of the village it was easy for
boys and girls to watch the cows, pigs, and sheep.

Through three centuries the village common has become
an integral part of many communities. Shaded by rough-
barked maples and graceful elms, it dozes calmly through
summer's heat and rests unperturbed through winter's
storms. Sometimes it is surrounded by an iron rail fence with
gray-granite posts at regular intervals. Most commons have
statues and memorials, erected in honor of heroes who have
given their lives for their country. Usually, there are a few
weather-stained oak or maple plank benches, where men of
years may sit and reminisce, or young mothers may visit
while their children play. Frequently, there is a watering
trough beside the common.

On the common was the bandstand, a circular affair, roofed
for protection, high above the ground so the music of the
Four Corners Cornet Band would spread over the crowd
that always came to the Wednesday evening concerts
throughout the summer. At one side was the village school
and on the other the white-spired, green-shuttered church.
Perhaps the Grange Hall and the Historical Society buildings also adjoined the common. Webster says, "Belonging or
pertaining to the community at large." That covers the technical aspect. Our definition for village common would be
"the heart of the community."

THE FAMILIAR CATBIRD IS A CHAP WITH CONTRARY characteristics. If politics be a major issue in the bird world, he has the qualifications for going far. He is loved, ridiculed, admired, and condemned; but he goes on serenely and confidently, knowing he has an exquisitely proportioned figure, a sleek, gray outfit, and a Beau Brummell air.

Galeoscoptes reminds one of some persons, who devote their energies to building a legend about themselves and playing to the public instead of going ahead with the workaday business of the world. He's a fellow of unpredictable moods. Sometimes he's gentle and meek and sings a song that proves he's a member in good standing of the mockingbird family. Again, a moment later, he's aggressive, scolding, and fault-finding, and utters harsh, nerve-jarring squawks and catcalls, which profane the quiet summer afternoon.

He is eminently qualified to be a court jester or a mimic. Like others of his family, he is an apt imitator; sometimes it seems as if he were taking a fiendish delight in caricaturing the melodies of other birds. On a tomato stake in the garden, after pruning and prinking his feathers for several minutes, he suddenly lifts his head and imitates a song sparrow. In a twinkling, he changes his mood and raucously echoes the grating call of a near-by blue jay.

He and his mate build their home in the thicket around the garden or in a bush at the edge of the woods. The nest is what one would expect, a hodge-podge scrap basket of coarse twigs, bits of paper, pieces of cloth, and bark. Here madame lays her four or five dark blue-green eggs and tends to the housekeeping, while her mate spends his time in the garden or the shrubbery. On the whole, we are in favor of Galeoscoptes. He has his irritating points, but philosophers tell us it takes all kinds to make a world. When he sings his own glorious song—a beautiful, long melody—he compensates for his antics and jesting.

*T*HERE ARE THOSE WHO DO NOT CHOOSE TO HOE. UNFOR-
tunately, those who do not choose to hoe sometimes
have no choice.

Those who believe that hoeing is a gentle art know that
certain conditions are necessary for the highest enjoyment of
both the material and the aesthetic aspects. The soil must be
soft and in good tilth; a plethora of turf clumps and fist-sized
stones turns delightful exercise into monotonous drudgery.
The understanding man hoes frequently, to maintain that
cushiony, friable layer of mellow topsoil.

The artist with a hoe insists on a lightweight tool of excel-
lent quality. The blade must be sharp and the corners must
be kept square for precision work around the beans, melons,
and corn. Such a hoe is as far removed from the dull-edged,
plebeian barn hoe as a manure spreader is from a stylish,
fringed-top surrey.

Artists are temperamental. Some prefer to work in the
dew-fresh morning, assembling thoughts for the day's work.
Others prefer to grind out the daily grist and then do their
hoeing in the cool of the evening, while the hermit thrush
sings his vespers from the edge of the woodland. Either way,
the artist with a hoe gets his satisfaction as the cool, moist
soil is stirred to freshness.

The Ell

*T*HERE IS A VOGUE FOR FUNCTIONAL ARCHITECTURE, AND in the main it has much to commend it. Doubtless, our housing styles have much of the Topsy philosophy, although experience has held out a restraining hand. As we read of glass-sided houses, heat under the floors, and flat roofs for sun bathing, the future seems destined to be a period of change in house styles—as in cars, planes, and robot bombs.

Nevertheless, the ell of the Northern farmstead will continue to have a functional purpose for a long time to come. There are those who smile at the thought of connecting the house where human beings live with the barn that shelters animals. One could mention that, in pioneer days on the frontier, the abode of the family cow, pig, and chickens frequently adjoined the family's own living room. There are, indeed, places in the world today where human beings and their beasts and birds live a more or less communal life.

The ell is a compromise. It is a series of rooms or sheds, each with a purpose. Urban dwellers without rural experience cannot know the peaceful comfort of going under cover from the farm kitchen to the tie-up on days when cold autumn rains are lashing the earth, when blizzardy storms whirl over field and wood, or when the snow lies deep and drifted after a norther.

The ell is a good thing. A farmer can walk from the regular kitchen to the back kitchen, through the woodshed, the carriage shed, the toolroom, the farm shop, and directly into the barn. Somehow, the ell binds the whole farm into a unit. It gives a sense of cozy security and protected unity. On a farm the heart of living is intimately bound with all the activities connected with the care of animals. The ell is a comfortable link between the home for the family and the home of the animals that depend on the farmer's care.

*T*HE TWO-SEATED DEMOCRAT IS A PART OF AMERICAN tradition. It did not have the cozy intimacy of the top buggy nor the style and zip of the fringed-top surrey. But many a city man who drives a car with three- or four-score horsepower magically concealed in a small space before him can remember the sturdy, utilitarian, two-seated democrat.

It was a wagon of many uses. On Sundays, Father, Mother, and four children could comfortably ride to the white church in the village. On Saturday evenings, when the family went to the general store for the week's groceries, notions, and a dime's worth of hard candies apiece for the children, there was room beneath the seats for the eggs, butter, and perhaps some fruits and vegetables for special customers. With the rear seat removed, the democrat was strong enough to carry a barrel of Baldwins or Northern Spies and a couple of sacks of Green Mountains to Uncle Barzoola and Aunt Hezekiah.

To many a farm lad this was the best of the farm vehicles. Likely enough, it was in the democrat that he was first permitted to drive alone to the village. It was probably the democrat that Father let him take when he was old enough to drive to Long Pond for a day's fishing. On a rainy day, one Morgan mare was hitched in the shafts and the other led behind, as he took them to the blacksmith shop to have their shoes reset. And on that red-letter day in the fall when the family went to the County Cattle Show, it was the democrat that carried them all, with boxes and hampers of lunch stowed beneath the seats.

It wasn't much to look at—just a set of wheels, a low box body, and two plain seats with leather cushions. But many are those who remember the sturdy wagon that rolled along the dusty roads behind a jogging horse.

F. W. Went

IN THE DAYS WHEN FARMS IN THE NORTHEAST WERE nearly self-sufficiency units, shrewd farmers had a recipe for a farm. It must have meadowland for hay, fields for grain, a wood lot, and an upland pasture. Each part fitted into the economic scheme. The upland pasture was important because it furnished feed from the middle of May until frost time for cows and neat stock, for sheep and lambs, colts, and the horses on days when they were not used for farm work.

The upland pasture is often studded with weather-grayed boulders and lichen-covered ledge outcroppings. Sprawling green patches of juniper bushes form an irregular pattern on the hillside. There are clumps of gray birches. In one corner, where a never-failing spring bubbles from the ground and flows into a moss-covered wooden trough, there is an area of high-bush blueberries, which mean juicy pies in late July and jars of the blue-black fruit for the cellar cupboard.

Here and there are masses of pink pasture roses, forming bright spots of color against gray rocks and sun-tanned grasses. Clumps of sheep laurel hold their stiff spikes aloft; and when goldenrod time comes coveys of the yellow blooms burst forth along the stone-wall fences. Over the stone walls lean alders, pasture pine, and scrub oaks. Beneath the wall is the home of Wejack, the philosophical, bewhiskered chuck, who always seems to get to his den a few yards ahead of the farm collie. In the highest corner is the maple grove, with its dilapidated sugar house. The shade of the trees is welcome to the stock on a hot day.

The pasture itself? There's grass—a surprising amount. Among the boulders and between patches of juniper, the stock finds the sparse, sweet grass. It isn't the type of pasture recommended by farm experts. One can't plow and harrow an area so steep and so filled with rocks; but the upland pasture will serve its purpose for a long time to come.

*W*EBSTER APTLY DEFINES THE VERB "TO FISH" AS "TO attempt to catch" and "to seek to obtain by artifice." But Webster does not go into the intangibles, and the true fisherman is concerned with more than frying-pan evidence. There are those who forthrightly say that a man goes fishing for the same reason that he plays golf; that is, to get away from the work that supports his family.

Men from eight to eighty enjoy fishing. One can't logically claim that it is the spirit of spring, for there is a group of fishermen who chop holes through the ice in midwinter and seek to obtain by artifice the denizens of pond and lake. Fishing is more than a seasonal urge; it has little to do with age; it is highly self-centered and introvert in character.

There's the deep peace and satisfaction of getting out of doors. It's good to feel the raw wind or the warm sun. It's good to be in old clothes and to wear a hat that has been a boon companion for years. It's good for a man to smell the earth and water and lift his eyes to stretching fields and wooded hills.

Naturally, anything as important as fishing is divided into camps of opinion. There are those who recoil in horror from using an earthworm and a willow pole. Some stand adamant for wet flies and some believe the piscatorial bill of rights means a dry fly. There are men who delight in scrambling along a brook's edge; while some prefer to wade in shallow, swift water. Others use a rowboat from which to cast plugs among the lily pads and water grasses. One group believes in trolling slowly and comfortably.

This is the way it should be. Fishing is too important for any bureau to regiment methods, equipment, and philosophies. Within a reasonable framework of reference, fishermen should have the privilege of regarding highly their own ideas and scoffing heartily at the ideas of others!

*T*HERE IS SOMETHING UNIQUE ABOUT A TRAIN WHISTLE. It is one of the links that bind a great, sprawling nation together.

Men and women now dwelling in teeming cities, whose ears are attuned to the rumbling roar of city traffic, jangling telephones, and the impatient blare of electrically motivated car horns, remember the train whistles that they heard when they lived in a more peaceful environment. It may have been on the broad, black-soil reaches of the Midwest, when the flier tore across the farmlands toward the distant metropolis. Many a farm lad has halted the team when turning over the brown slices of earth or when riding the hayrake, to watch the approach of the train and wave to the engineer. It may have been on the short-grass, lonely prairies or in the sandy-soiled, piney regions of the South.

Again, it may have been in the mountains and valleys of the Northeast, where the whistle echoed back and forth among the hills as the train puffed its way up steep grades, following the river valley as it wound in and out among the wooded heights. On rainy days and at night the long, lonesome, drawn-out whooo-whooo-whoo-whoo seemed to linger over fields and uplands. On the branch lines, farmers and villagers knew when Local 67 arrived at Johnson's Crossing. They would look at their watches. "She's late, but she can make it up on the level stretch going into Centerville."

No one knows how many farm lads, during the last century, have lain in their beds and listened to the whistle as the lighted train rushed through the black night. As they listened, they dreamed youth's dream of high adventure, and always the dream included the nerve-tingling anticipation that some day they would be on that train—riding to a future of accomplishment in the world of human affairs.

TIME WAS, BEFORE THE MOWING MACHINE WAS IN-vented, when a man's skill with snath and scythe was a matter of importance. The grass of the upland fields and low-lying meadows was cut by hand. The countryman can remember when a dozen men, one offset behind the other, cut their swaths across big fields in the early morning when dew was still on the grass.

Mowing by hand is an art. Those who have mastered the rhythmic precision of the process have an instinctive sense of timing and balance. The mower is as particular about his snath and scythe as is the artist about his fine-gauge instruments. The snath must "feel right" to the hands; the balance must suit, and the weight must match a man's muscle. A good farmer is as particular about his snath as he is about his axe. The scythe must be of good steel and take a fine edge.

To watch a master mower in action is to see the poetry of motion. Bent forward from the hips, neither too far nor too little, he swings his easy, calculated strokes. With the heel of the snath close to the ground, he lays windrows of sweet-scented grasses in parallel rows. With feet a few inches apart, he edges forward with steady, short steps. At intervals he pauses, rests the end of the snath on the turf, pulls a whetstone from the long, narrow pocket on the leg of his overalls, and renews the edge of the blade. With sure, long strokes the stone rings against the steel; then, with his thumb, the mower tests the renewed cutting edge.

Today the scythe is used for "trimming out." A day or two before haying gets under way, the farmer trims out around the buildings, around the gardens, and along the stone walls and fences. It isn't mowing by hand as the farmers of yesteryear knew it, but the countryman still enjoys the feel of his balanced outfit as the razor-sharp blade swishes through grass and clover.

*T*HE COUNTRYSIDE WOULD LACK PART OF ITS INTEREST without the busy chipmunk. Tamias is a cosmopolitan sort; he's at home in the farm dooryard or along the edges of the woodland. He delights in scampering along the uneven tops of weather-grayed stone walls and the top rail of hemstitch-patterned split fences. He bustles about with nervous activity throughout the season; but when the frost-touched days of fall arrive he's a veritable dynamo of action as he sprints hither and yon for the food he's caching against the time of snow and ice.

Tamias is a social chap. A favorite spot is the woodpile in the back yard. It offers security if Shep embarks on one of his frantic barking blitzkriegs, though Shep long ago decided he'd leave Tamias alone except for a bit of needed exercise.

A chipmunk can talk back. His animated, rapid-fire "chuck-chuck-chuck" reveals his feelings. To Shep or other annoyers he speaks with intense emotion. His explosive chatter reveals anger over the interruption of a squirrel's work and a tinge of contempt for those who think they can include him in their diet. But if the day has gone well, if the weather is good and prospects for winter food are average or better, Tamias chatters pleasantly and gossipingly, as a man works about the farmyard.

In late autumn, when the Frost King sends his legions to lock the earth, the chipmunk goes into his burrow for semi-hibernation. On mild, sunny days of midwinter he may come out for an observation tour. Most of the time, however, he sleeps. Occasionally, he has a meal from the store of nuts and seeds in his bulky, leafy nest at the end of his burrow. On a mellow March day, when one can almost feel a south breeze unlocking the land, Tamias suddenly appears. Then the countryman knows that winter's reign is ended.

Raking After

A HAND-PULLED BULL RAKE IS NOT A TOOL THAT AP-
peals to a fourteen-year-old. A lad who enjoys
swinging an axe or hiking long miles with a rifle considers
raking after one of the worst jobs in the season's calendar.

There are a number of reasons why pulling a bull rake is
not a glamorous job. First, it is steady, hard work, especially
if the man pitching on is a fast worker who likes to lift an
entire stack in one pitchforkful. That keeps a fellow on the
hustle. Holding the point of the bound-together handles in
one hand and grasping with the other the bar between the
handles where the space begins to widen, while the hay is
rapidly increasing on the foot-length teeth, a lad has to make
hurried trips to the nearest stacks to get rid of his load.

In the second place, one has to watch the ground all the
time when he's raking after by hand. The man who is building the load has an occasional moment to look out over the
field or meadow and know the rest of the world is still there.
Besides, there's a psychological satisfaction in being up in
the air. The ground is a very ordinary, prosaic place. Even
pitching on, hard work as it is, is infinitely preferable to
raking after. A young, young man can test his strength
against a forkful. He can shout "Here it comes," though only
part of it arrives.

Raking after is definitely a boy's work—and boys have
always preferred men's work. The bull rake grows heavier
and clumsier as the long hours wear on. The pointed teeth
catch on hummocks and tufts. The man pitching on is un-
questionably leaving more and more for the one who rakes
after. There is only one thing that makes raking after en-
durable on a hot, sticky summer's day. When the last load
is on and the men wait as the scatterings are pulled together,
a boy knows that the water in the meadow swimming hole
is cool and refreshing.

REPORTS FROM THE FARM FRONT SAY THAT ONCE again cream is being churned into butter. Attics are being searched; that dusty space above the woodshed is getting cleaned at last; the countryman is untangling a mass of old chicken wire, barrels, baskets, and broken tools. A churn has become a cherished thing.

We have heard of city housekeepers who use egg beaters to churn butter in a bowl. But, some years ago, churning was a major operation among the weekly tasks. The milk was put into tall, cylindrical tin cans, about three feet tall and one foot in diameter, where the cream rose to the top, inches thick, like a mammoth tiddlywink. From a small faucet at the bottom of each can the skim milk was drawn off. Then the heavy, golden cream was put into an earthen jug in the pantry. Here it was kept a few days to "ripen."

On churning day the squat, sturdy churn was set on the kitchen table and half-filled with warm water to warm the wooden sides and paddle. The gray jug of cream was placed on the back of the kitchen range to warm the contents. When Mother felt that the temperatures were right, the water was drained from the churn and the cream was put in. Then a farm lad started turning the crank.

Sometimes the butter "came" easily and quickly. On other occasions it was stubborn and slow. The paddles went around —slosh, slosh, slosh. Chunks of butter began to form. The slosh-slosh changed to ker-plunk, ker-plunk. The plug was pulled and the fresh, gold-specked buttermilk was drawn off.

The butter was put into a big wooden bowl and worked until all liquid was forced out. After salt was added, the butter was molded into pound prints with a clover-leaf design. Wrapped in butter paper, it was stored for future use or for trading at the general store. It is good to know that churns have returned to a place of importance. The song of the paddles in the heavy cream is a cheerful tune.

IREFLIES ARE LILLIPUTIAN LAMPLIGHTERS. MR. WEB-
ster's prosaic and succinct definition of the on-again,
off-again light givers as "small, elongated and flattened soft-
bodied beetles producing a soft, intermittent light from the
lower abdomen" covers sufficient technical details. It is not,
however, satisfactory to those who delight in the myriad soft,
intermittent gleams that dot the darkness of a summer's
night.

Photinus lampyridae is a debonair, determined fellow.
With six legs and two antennae, which branch from his head
like the horns of an old-time Texas steer, he is built on the
lines of a low-slung racing car. The long, slender wings ex-
tend from the shoulders to beyond the rear of the body. The
posterior end would be a very acceptable model for a "tear-
drop" rear of the motor car of tomorrow. The bits of light
are caused by the luminous material of the lower abdomen,
revealed when the wings are lifted in flight, shut off momen-
tarily when they are close to the body.

Fireflies favor the darkness of a quiet summer night. In the
early evening, when the whippoorwills are calling from the
stone wall along the pasture lane and a late-retiring robin
broadcasts a few chirps from the old August Sweet tree by
the icehouse, the lamplighters start forth on their rounds.
Sometimes, just before a storm, when the early night is particularly dark and the air is heavy and oppressive, it seems
as if legions of reserves have been called into action. The
meadows and fields are crisscrossed, dotted, and starred by
flashing points, as the thousands of beetles swoop and turn,
climb and dive. Fireflies are the lamplighters of field and
meadow—seasonal evidence of the "good old summertime."

Scarecrow

*T*HERE ARE A NUMBER OF PLEASANT AND SATISFYING aspects of scarecrows. They have solid historical tradition. The construction allows for individuality and initiative. They amuse and entertain the crows. Feathered friends do so much for humanity that it seems proper and fitting for us to do something in return.

Building a scarecrow is an absorbing task for a rainy day. The farm shop is a comfortable environment for making what Mr. Webster defined as "an object, usually suggesting a human figure, set up to frighten crows; hence, anything terrifying without danger." The purpose, admittedly, is an object to terrify; but the countryman is likely to shift his point of emphasis from terror to originality. And there's rarely any danger about a scarecrow, unless it gets tangled with the cultivator.

A good scarecrow requires thought, time, and a sense of artistic rightness. A pair of old pants, a coat, and a vest serve as foundation. From then on, a scarecrow accumulates the details that mark the master craftsman. Clothes should be stuffed to provide lifelike lines. A hat is needed, not a cap. Whoever saw a farmer working in a cap? A cap is quite in fashion for the Saturday evening trip to town, but not for field work. A face made on a white pine board is a nice touch, especially if it is decorated with a handle-bar moustache.

A man who has pride in his work can always add furbelows and frills that distinguish the superior from the mediocre. The whole point is, if one is going to build an effect to terrify "without danger" and knows in his heart that it doesn't terrify, he should give our black-feathered friends a chance to rest on a sturdy, carefully planned, artistically designed affair that is worthy of Corvus brachyrhynchos.

41

*T*HERE IS SOMETHING SATISFYING ABOUT A FARM SHOP on a rainy day in midsummer—partly, perhaps, because one is glad of a leisurely day in the midst of haying. Or it may be that the steady fall of rain on the roof, the low-lying nimbus clouds, and the soft gray light over the upland fields and valley meadows create an atmosphere that relaxes.

The countryman is justifiably proud of the farm shop. The man on the farm cannot trot to the neighborhood hardware store or to the local man of all trades. The farmer is his own mender. Therefore, the farm shop, over the years—or the generations—has accumulated an assortment of tools. They hang from pegs and spikes and slots above the stained and nicked bench of solid maple planks; sledge hammers, crowbars, and shovels stand in the corners. The bench itself is a mass of odds and ends. A two-man crosscut saw dangles from a brace on the wall. Under the bench there is a heterogeneous jumble of pieces of broken chains, sections of harness, scraps of lumber, and old buckets. From the rafters overhead hang pails and burlap bags, old snaths, a sickle, baskets, and traces of seed corn. In one corner is the small, one-cover, rusty, rotund stove; around the floor are decrepit chairs, boxes, old rubber boots, grease cans, and nail kegs. The casual visitor might think the place the apogee of confusion, but the farmer knows where everything is—or, at least, can put his hands on anything with a minimum of search.

Not the least satisfying is the smell. It's a wholesome, nostril-tingling aroma, compounded of old leather, rubber, sawdust, cobwebs, an old horse blanket, lumber, good honest dirt on the floor, needled with the penetrating pungency of creosote and fertilizer. Of course, there is work to be done. A good farmer has his rainy-day jobs; but it's unhurried, pleasant work in the farm shop on a rainy summer day.

*T*HE SUMMER PASTURE IS OFTEN A FEW MILES FROM home—usually, on the side of a mountain or stretching across an upland ridge. Ordinarily several farmers combine to drive their stock to and from the summer grazing. The man who rents the grazing, for a dollar or so a month per head, salts the cattle; but a good husbandman likes to keep his eye on his own, and the Sunday afternoon trip to the mountain pasture has become an accepted and enjoyable part of summer's routine in many farm families.

A generation and more ago, some farm families went to the mountain pasture after church services were over. Often several families went together and had a picnic lunch in a grove at the foot of the mountain road that led to the upland grazing areas. The two-seated democrats were well laden with youngsters, and under the seats were baskets of good food. After a ride of an hour or more, lunch was eaten; then, while the womenfolk sat and visited on the red-and-black checked lap robes, the men and the young folks climbed the mountain trail to see the cattle.

It was thrilling to see the Jerseys, Guernseys, Durhams, Holsteins, and Ayrshires come running for their salt, sure of a treat from their human friends. As they lapped the salt with rough tongues, the men looked them over with judicious eyes, comparing notes on breeds and animals. Good husbandmen, who knew their cattle, they exemplified the scriptural admonition—"the eye of the master fatteneth the flock." As the sun dropped lower and shadows inched out from the woods into grassy openings, the group moved slowly down the gullied, bouldered road toward home and chores. The cattle, their craving satisfied, drifted toward the spring and their supper's grazing. All was well in the highland pasture. The stock had been "salted" again.

HUMBLE TOOLS HAVE ALWAYS BEEN MAN'S GOOD friends. Whether in time-mossed lands of the East or on new and rapidly expanding frontiers, simple tools have played a major role. The axe, the rifle, and the hoe were tools that helped push this nation across the eastern wall, through the river valleys, across the grass-padded plains and over the divide to the western ocean. The axe, the rifle, and the hoe have had songs sung in their honor; but little has been said and sparse has been the praise for another humble, sturdy tool.

Spades and shovels have made history and brought the comforts of civilization. They have helped to make beds for the rails that span a continent; they have helped build great turnpikes and humble dirt roads; they dug the "Big Ditch" that linked the Hudson and the Great Lakes and speeded the settling of a new nation. Machine monsters dig ditches today; but, on the farm, shovels and spades still play important roles.

There are degrees of honor among farm shovels, but the farmer's pride is a long-handled, sharp-pointed one. This he uses for digging postholes, for bringing loads of gravel for the farm drive. It is kept in the tool-room, oiled and clean. The boys are not allowed to use it; for a good farmer knows that when a man has a tool that just fits his hands such a tool must be cherished and cared for.

Corn Chowder

*T*HE CORN-CHOWDER CONNOISSEUR WILL RECOGNIZE THE significance of the word "chowder" when he knows that it comes from a French word meaning kettle, or pot. Only the initiated realize that the sole genuine, history-proved, traditionally accepted method of making real corn chowder is to cook it in an old iron kettle, which sits in a hole ordinarily occupied by one of the stove covers. They know, too, that a good, big, wood-burning kitchen stove has three rows of stove lids of two each. To make corn chowder that's something more than a mess of potatoes, onions, and corn in a quart or two of liquid, these stove lids are essential; for to reach the heights of which it is capable, chowder must be started slowly and permitted to gather momentum in flavorful lusciousness as the hours tick by.

First, try out two or three slices of salt pork, with a few streaks of lean marbling the white goodness; cut the nut-brown, crisp slices into small cubes and place them, with the tried-out fat, in the bottom of the kettle sitting in one of the middle-row holes. Cut up two or three onions and fuse them with the pork scraps. Add some half-boiled potatoes and mix the three ingredients. After a half hour or so, add two quarts of whole milk and a can or two of cream-style corn. Little by little, the chowder warms. When all is blended, move the kettle to a front hole over the crackling fire. Stir it constantly, tasting frequently. Never let corn-chowder boil. When it is piping hot, place the kettle in one of the rear holes to keep warm. Then, and only then, add salt and pepper to suit.

Corn chowder should not entirely cool before the final re-heating. Made right after dinner, it is in its prime for supper. Served with plenty of crackers to crumble into the savory bowlful, where a good pat of butter floats on top, it's a supper dish that the countryman looks forward to as he comes through the ell after the day's chores are done.

*T*IME WAS, BEFORE AUTOMOBILES AND TRUCKS SUP-
planted lithe trotters, leggy pacers, and heavy work
horses, when the brook passages were an integral part of the
rural scene.

They were in New England, beside bridges across swift-
running, clear-water brooks with bottoms of clean sand and
white pebbles; they were in the Middle West, where winding
cottonwood-shaded creeks meandered leisurely through the
depressions of wide fields; they were in the middle and lower
South, beside bridges that spanned water flowing between
banks of reddish clay. It seems logical to ask, Why have
bridges at all if people preferred to drive through the water?
But in the winter, in spring freshet season, and after heavy
rains, when brooks and creeks swelled to miniature rivers,
the bridges were necessary.

Countrymen drove through the brook in hot weather for
three reasons. It gave the horses a chance to drink; it was
good for their hoofs to be soaked in the mud and water; it
gave a chance to swell the fellies, so that they would stay
tight to the wheel rims.

To a ten-year-old lad the brook passage counted for
more than these utilitarian benefits. Under the splintered,
weather-grayed planks of the bridge was a shady, dim oasis
of enchantment. One could climb along the mossy boulders
of the abutments and see brightly speckled trout darting for
shelter. There was often a phoebe's home to explore and
dozens of mud daubers' nests. Sometimes one found a fresh-
water clam, with the always present chance of a pearl—which
never seemed to materialize. At length, Grandfather would
say: "Well, Son, the Jerseys will be waiting for us," and a boy
reluctantly left his explorations. Yes, brook passages are good
for thirst, hoofs, and fellies; but a boy knows they are good
for other purposes too.

NEW ENGLAND'S STONE WALLS MAKE A PATCHWORK-quilt pattern of the landscape. They are the weather-grayed, lichen-covered threads that run along country roads, climb upland pastures, and meander over brows of low mountains. They encompass small mowing fields and circle fertile meadows.

Over them lean birches and alders and sumacs. Along the tops scamper chipmunks and red squirrels. On them the cock ruffed grouse stands and sends his drumming defiance reverberating through woodland aisles. Beneath the walls by the farm garden and across the mowing field, the wily woodchuck makes his den and tantalizes Shep, the collie. Through frost-heaved gaps the wild folk of forest and swamp make their regular rounds and use the openings as tollgate stations to collect news of the area.

A century and a half ago, "wall making" was a regular part of the farm's operations. Whenever a day was available between seasonal tasks, the yoke of oxen was hitched to the stoneboat and more wall was built. New England pioneers cleared their fields of rocks and used them for boundaries. Building a good wall was a craftsman's task. Foundations had to be dug below frost line; big rocks went at the bottom, the small at the top. "A rod a day for two men and a yoke" was a standard measurement.

Through the years, the stone walls have been a hallmark of the region. In many places thin-soiled fields that pioneers once cleared have reverted to woodland and hidden the walls from the casual eye. For many generations they will stand, through blizzard and storm, meeting the seasons in their cycles—a memorial to the men and boys of yesteryear who built a region's fences.

THE GRAY BIRCH IS A HUMBLE, UNPRETENTIOUS SORT OF tree—a poor but worthy cousin of the glamorous white birch and the aldermanic yellow birch. Like most of the humble, service-giving forms of life in nature, it is found over an extensive area. Betula populifolia doesn't grow very tall. A gray birch that is more than eight inches in diameter is conspicuous among its peers. But gray birches are a friendly, everyday sort of tree. They do not aspire to the dignity of the massive oaks, the austerity of the smooth-barked beeches, or the rugged individualism of the rough-barked sugar maples. The grays tuck themselves into the crevices and corners. They are found in clumps along the stone walls of the upland pasture, in the half-open spaces of the wood lot, in boulder-studded ravines. Along the back-country roads they mix in casual good neighborliness with sumac, dogwood, and alders.

The grays have many names. In various localities they are called poverty birch, poplar birch, paper birch, or old-field birch. In spite of the commonplace names, these trees have charm. The triangular leaves with acuminate tips and doubly serrate margins; the gracefully slender, pendulous catkins; the grayish-white bark with heavy black markings running downward at the branch junctions—all these give the grays a certain long-wearing beauty.

The countryman likes to chop the grays for the fireplace. The wood, which is easy to work, is one of the few woods that burn without much seasoning. The pulpy stumps make good home sites for the chickadees; and the downies and the nuthatches delight to hunt for grubs in the weathered soft-ness. Gray birches are common, but these Marthas of nature's family serve faithfully and well.

Red-flannel Hash

*T*HERE IS NO RECORD THAT THE RED MEN TAUGHT THE early colonists to make red-flannel hash. The origin of the bulgy beet is shrouded in mystery—a fitting subject for a doctor's thesis in horticulture. One can only hope that the Indians, who knew corn, beans, and squashes, also knew the beet.

It is unfortunate that the word "hash" has become associated with this combination. The word has fallen into some disrepute. "Mother's mystery" is not enigmatic; it is good, solid, everyday grub.

Red-flannel hash, however, is on a different plane. It is an Oriental-looking, taste-tantalizing dish. Its color is exciting. It has allure and snap. A frying pan full of it on the kitchen stove sends a nostril-tickling aroma through the room. As a man comes through the woodshed with the milk pails on his arm, he inhales the smell and a smile lights his face. What better reward for a long day's work digging potatoes or picking apples?

How to make it? Heat an old iron spider on a wood-burning stove. Fry a few slices of bacon until they are crisp and break into small bits. Chop a dozen cooked beets into small pieces; mix in two or three boiled potatoes and two chopped onions. The countryman, who is meticulous regarding certain culinary points, says that correct red-flannel hash is 85 per cent beet, 10 per cent potato, 3 per cent onion, and 2 per cent bacon; and that never under any circumstances should it include meat (other than bacon), gravy, or extraneous vegetables. Serve it piping hot with yellow corn-meal muffins and green-tomato pickles. For dessert, a wedge of deep-dish apple pie, a piece of old sharp cheese, and a glass of cold, creamy milk are acceptable.

Armstrong R...

CUTTING THE LATE ROWEN IS A PLEASANT FALL TASK ON the farm. There's a sense of urgency in regular haying season; during hot July days the farm family stretches every sinew to get the crop quickly under cover. But when rowen time comes, there's a different spirit over the land. The rush of the season's work is past; main crops are in. The rowen, six or eight inches tall, is tender and nutritious fodder. Many a countryman prizes his last cutting of clover and timothy as the hay for his best cows or for a favorite horse.

Very likely, light frosts have lain on it; but rowen also knows the blessed touch of early fall rains after the dryness and heat of August. The farmer goes at the cutting of his rowen leisurely. The short grass has a nostril-tingling fragrance. In the mellow September sunshine it cures quickly, and the hard-to-describe but unforgettable aroma of sweet drying hay fills the air. It is easy to mow because of its short length. In the same field where the horses leaned hard against their collars for the main cutting, they now pull the singing mowing machine at a brisk, easy clip.

On many farms, rowen time is when Mother and the girls enjoy tramping the loads in the hayrack. Father isn't so particular about building a big load; an extra trip means little when there's a small harvest and time's not pressing. On quiet, brooding days, when the sun's rays seem to soak into brown stubble and the September haze lies over the upland pastures and mountain slopes, rowen time is a good period in the farm calendar. It's the last crop from the hayfield. Rowen time means the end of the harvest season. When this crop is safely under cover, the countryman is ready for the frost-bound months ahead.

MAIN STREET ON SATURDAY NIGHT IN THOUSANDS OF towns is a good cross section of the heart of America—where countrymen meet their peers.

The Saturday evening trip is a cherished, leisurely part of country living. Father and the boys finish the chores a little early. The baked beans, sweet tomato pickle, hot cornbread, deep-dish apple pie and glasses of cold, rich milk are all the tastier because of the trip to come. Mother and the girls wash the dishes while Father cuts what he calls the "best-growing crop on the farm," and changes into his second-best suit.

The eggs, perhaps a few bushels of fruit, and—yes—a carton of pound prints of butter are loaded into the car trunk. Urbanites would be amazed if they knew the number of good farmers who still plan to take something to sell when they go to town. There are still many stores where the sign announces truly: General Merchandise—Groceries, Hardware, Grain, Clothing, Notions.

But the real spirit of Main Street Saturday night has nothing to do with marts of trade. It is the friendliness of neighboring with others, the catching up on the news of the countryside, the inevitable discussions of crops and weather and livestock. It is the political discussions, all the way from who will be the next road agent to who will be the next president. It is the freedom of speech; the certainty of worth of another's opinion; the give and take of free men who fight hard and honestly; the belief that life can be made better. Main Street Saturday night is a great public forum of a great nation.

Picklin' Time

*T*HERE'S A TANTALIZING, SPICY, SWEET-SOUR SMELL coming from the farm kitchen. On a sunny September morning when the countryman is cutting the late rowen, when blue haze hovers on the mountains across the valley, and all earth lies quietly in the fruition of autumn, Mother begins to make the season's batch of pickles.

Picklin' time is an important date on the season's calendar. What would home-baked beans be like without pickles? Could one be expected to enjoy a juicy roast of pork on a blizzardy January noon without their tart, biting goodness? And with the fried potatoes for everyday supper what goes better than a generous helping of green-tomato pickles?

There are all kinds of pickles: green tomato, chutney, beet relish, pickled baby beets, corn relish, sweet mustard pickles, sweet ripe cucumber, bread-and-butter pickles, and others. Each has its place; each is a natural companion for some good dish. The chief point is—it's picklin' time. The pungent, penetrating, tantalizing aroma is all through the house.

It spreads into the woodshed where a twelve-year-old lad is stacking chunks of solid oak and maple against the time of cold, and it makes him stop, sniff in appreciation, and smile in anticipation. Mother bends over the bubbling kettle on the stove and inhales critically. Is it strong enough of this or too strong of that? Her menfolk have preferences. As the countryman comes into the kitchen for a midmorning drink of cold water, he whiffs the air with a commendable degree of authority. "I always like picklin' time," he says. "Smells good."

By Ewing Galloway, N. Y.

By Ewing Galloway, N. Y.

Armstrong Ro

Armstrong Roberts

Stacking Beans

*W*HEN NIGHTS ARE CRISP AND FROSTY AND THE FIRST thin silvery sheet of ice forms on the watering trough in the barnyard, it is time to stack the beans. Of the several varieties of beans for baking, some prefer the rich, mellow red kidneys; some, the mealy, crunchy yellow eyes; others, the small, nutty pea beans. The farmer knows that, whatever the variety, the stacking of his winter's supply for the Saturday-night baked beans is an important autumnal task.

Taking a light axe, he goes to pasture or wood lot for a gray birch of just the right size. It must be from two to three inches in diameter and studded with small sturdy branches. The branches are cut off about eight inches from the trunk; the base end is cleared to a height of two feet. The tree is cut off so that the total height is about seven feet. Around the tree, with its dozens of prickly, wooden quills, the beans are to be stacked.

The base is jammed into a hole made with a crowbar; a few flattish stones are placed under the branches around the small trunk. Then, handful by handful, the bean stack is built, with root ends next the pole. Round and round the stack the farmer works, fitting the roots tightly against the pole, pushing and pressing the pods and dried leaves together. There's an art to building a good stack of beans, as there is to building a load of hay. The same rule applies: keep the center lower than the outside edges.

Through days of mellow fall warmth and nights when the black frost touches field, pasture, and meadow, the beans stand on the stacks, drying out for their destiny in earthen pots in steady, slow ovens. Then, before the storms of late autumn begin, the farmer moves them to the edge of the barn floor. Some windy December day, he will pull them from the stacks, spread the plants in a layer on the barn floor, and flail out the nuggets.

Shelling Corn

*T*HERE ARE, OF COURSE, WORSE JOBS THAN SHELLING corn. Cleaning the hen house, for example, has just about the lowest possible rating in a teen-ager's list. But at the turn of the century, when Northeastern farmers still raised fields of dent and flint instead of driving to the feed store for a load of grain, shelling corn was one of those jobs that had to be done.

Although some farmers had small gasoline engines to supply power, on most farms the boys furnished the power. Turning the crank on the sheller was a good deal like turning the grindstone. It took an unconscionable amount of turning to get the desired results.

The first hour wasn't too bad. Likely enough, it was a gray, stormy, late-autumn day. Shelling corn was a clean task, compared with cleaning the hen house, and more active than oiling the heavy work harnesses. For a while it was rather fun to see the husked ears with their symmetrical lines of kernels go into the gears and to watch the battered metal basket slowly fill with the nuggets of grain. If Father hadn't put the day's stint so high, a fellow could get by; but, by and by, turning the crank became a monotonous, tiring chore.

That's when a lad began to think seriously of Grandfather's stories. In his day, they ground corn and cob together, and a treadmill powered by a steady horse furnished the energy. Grandfather always claimed that corn and cob meal meant sleek cattle. He didn't hold with modern ideas. A good treadmill with horsepower seemed a mighty logical method. When shelling corn was done by boy power, the grain bin and the kitchen wood box seemed to have one remarkable similarity: they were hard to keep filled.

F. W. Wen

*T*HERE COMES A RAINY SATURDAY IN THE FALL THAT means a certain job to farm lads. To avoid it, boys have been known to volunteer to clean out the old sawdust in the icehouse or even to clean out the hen house. But fate is inexorable, and the day arrives when the verdict is given. The harness must be washed and oiled before winter sets in.

After one gets started, it isn't too bad a job. By the time a crackling fire is started in the sheet-iron stove in the farm workshop and a pail of water heated to temper the water in the battered tin tub, one is mentally conditioned for the hours ahead. First, the harness is taken apart and necessary repairs are made. Then the harness soaks for a while in the tub, with a handful of sal soda added to the water. As each leather part is removed, it is scrubbed with a stiff-bristled brush on a slanted scrubbing board, so that the water is returned to the tub. While the leather is still moist the harness oil is rubbed in. Then the metal parts are polished to pleasing brightness.

That's the technical side of the job. The other side has compensations. As one works over the traces, reins, breeching, backstraps, breast straps, saddle pieces, cruppers, checkreins, and hip straps, it's pleasant to listen to the snapping fire in the stove and the steady drumming of the cold rain on the roof. There's time to think of the continued story in the farm journal, the Grange supper that's coming next week, and the deer tracks by the meadow brook. As time wears into the afternoon and night begins to shut down early, it's a satisfaction to put the harnesses together and know they are ready for the months ahead. Washing and oiling harness is something like the conversations that precede a diplomatic conference. It's essential work, which has to be done before real tasks are undertaken.

*L*IKE THINGS AND PEOPLE WHO KEEP CLOSE TO THE wholesomeness of earth, the stoneboat is simple and honest. It is usually made of two or more planks, bolted together with crossbars. The front end is upturned, so that it will slide over the ground without catching on rocks and other obstacles. Perhaps, this plebeian, sturdy farm conveyance is called a "boat" because of the upturned prow. No carved figure adorns it—as was customary on the boats of the viking explorers and the whalers from Nantucket and New Bedford, built for distant voyages. However, the stoneboat plows the earthen sea as stanchly as the boats of yesteryear plowed the fields of water.

A good farmer is particular about his stoneboat. The planks must be of oak, maple, or ash, tough and strong to bear heavy loads. After the planks are cut in the local sawmill, they are soaked, in order that the front ends may be bent up. Local blacksmiths have made a reputation for building stoneboats as well as sleds and farm-wagon bodies, for blacksmiths are versatile craftsmen.

The name "stoneboat" declares the main purpose of this vehicle, which, for three centuries, on thousands of farms, has carried rocks and boulders from land that men wanted to clear. Stoneboats have helped in building the stone walls that surround fields, enclose pastures, and run along the winding country roads. They have borne the rocks that became foundations for homes and barns, churches and town halls. They have contributed toward building bases for the muddy spots of country roads and the abutments of bridges that arch over rivers and brooks. Battered and splintered, unpretentious but useful, they have had their share in the making of a nation.

Farm Chimneys

*T*HERE ARE SMOKE BANNERS IN THE SKY, THESE FROSTY mornings—banners that tell of peace and quiet routine in the countryside. From the weathered, dull-red chimneys streaked with soot, the smoke from farmhouse kitchen stoves spirals upward into the still, cold air.

The smoke tells a story to the countryman who glances at it as he goes with full milk pails from the barn to the milk-house. He built the fire an hour ago. He knows that it is a good fire. Each winter he gathers a pile of kindling wood from the smaller, dead branches of pine trees. "Nothing like pine kindling" is a rural proverb. The resinous softwood gives a quick, intense heat to start the solid pieces of maple, oak, and birch.

Now the womenfolk are working in the kitchen, getting a breakfast on which a man can do a day's work in the open air. The brisk fire is sending up a good volume of smoke. For a few yards above the dark top bricks of the chimney it rises straight into the air. Along the outside edges of the column there are little curlicues and wisps that form circling eddies. Sometimes a stray bit separates from the stream and evaporates into nothingness. At the top of the pearl-gray banner, the smoke may veer toward the east and gradually disappear. The farmer looks, notes the wind is from the west, and counts on a good day.

Time was when smoke from a cabin chimney was a cheering sign to weary pioneer travelers. Thoreau called it "The standard raised over some rural homestead. When its fine column rises above the forest, like an ensign, some human life has planted itself." These prewinter mornings, when the farmsteads are preparing for the months of cold, the smoke banners are good omens—omens of peace and plenty.

F. W. Went

$\mathcal{M}$R. WEBSTER, SUCCINCT AND DIRECT AS USUAL, SAYS that to plow is "to turn up, break up, or trench; to proceed laboriously." As any farmer will tell you, there is plowing and there is plowing. In a field studded with stones, seen and unseen, plowing becomes a sort of wrestling match, with the odds favoring the stones. When the share strikes a hidden stone, the chain connecting the clevis to the whiffle-tree slackens and, because of some mysterious law of higher mathematics or obfuscated physics, the handles jump up and catch a man under the ribs. At such moments, a Northeastern farmer knows why some of his ancestors didn't look back at the upland pastures and stone walls as they headed for the black soil of the Ohio Valley.

But there's another kind of plowing. When the soil is free of obstruction and is moist enough for the jointer to cut cleanly through the sod and the brown ribbons roll steadily off the moldboard, there's a fascinating rhythm as the horses pull steadily ahead. The countryman will tell you that a good team makes up a major part of plowing. Fast walkers are an irritation and put too much of a strain on a man's arms; yet, if the horses are too slow, the work becomes monotonous.

Plowing in the fall is good work. It gives a man a chance to hear the blue jays screaming in the beeches and the crows calling from the maple grove. While the team is taking a breather, he can hear the chickadees in the gray birches on the other side of the pasture wall. As he lifts his eyes to the hills across the valley and sees the brown of the oak leaves blending with the green of the pines and hemlocks, he is glad that he lives in the country, where a man's eyes can rise to beauty. Science says that straight furrows are not the thing, and that the farmer is a conservationist; but he's glad that he can still plow. Plowing is satisfactory work, whether in a straight line or following the natural contour of the land.

F. W. Wentz

Mail-order Time

*W*HEN THE HARVEST SEASON DRAWS TOWARD A CLOSE; when barns are packed with fodder; when the corncribs are stuffed to overflowing; when the farmhouse cellar is filled with potatoes, apples, and root vegetables; and when the shelves are lined with jams, fruits, jellies, and pickles, it is mail-order time.

Many men and women living in cities and large towns know the thrill of mail-order time. Shopping is a great American institution, whether in a crossroads country store, at a mammoth department store, or from a mail-order catalogue. One joy of mail-order shopping is that the shopper can take his time, keep changing his mind, compare, revise, and discuss.

In many farm families, each member makes out his own list. A stormy fall evening is a favorite time. Chores are done; the livestock is fed and bedded for the night. Supper is over, dishes are washed, and around the big kitchen table with its red-checkered cloth the family studies and ponders. Sleet and rain may pound against the windows; but here in the big, thick catalogues is another world. The illustrations are tempting; the colors are gay and exciting; the writing is terse and appealing. The writers of the advertisements may not have had technical courses in two-dollar words, but they know human nature.

Around tables in kitchens and living rooms, in friendly, battered Morris chairs and in Boston rockers with their white tidies, men and women, boys and girls are poring over the catalogues. That's America—earning money and spending it. We don't need to worry too much about the American standard of living as long as people like to buy things both to get efficient service and to satisfy a love of beauty.

A GENERATION AGO, WHEN COUNTRY ROADS WERE STILL used by horses, farm wagons, buggies, and fringed-top surreys, a farmer might spend a week or more during the fall on the roads—working out part of his taxes.

Fall work on the country roads followed a definite pattern. Each year, the town planned to gravel a mile or two of dirt road. A gravel road was a distinct upward step in the scale of transportation facilities. In late fall, with crops under cover and the winter's supply of wood stacked in the shed, there were three or four weeks before ground freezing. Then farmers who wished to do so might work out their taxes.

The standard unit was the two-horse dumpcart, which hauled a cubic yard of gravel. A farmer fortunate enough to own a gravel bank sold the material to the town for about ten cents a yard. All day long, the teams drove into the pasture where the bank was located; the shovelers quickly filled the cart, and the team started off for the spot where the road was being finished.

The technical part of road building in those days was simple: a high-crowned roadbed, deep side ditches; stones and rocks in the known mudholes; thank-you-ma'ams on the hills. But working out the taxes was much more than adding another section of gravel road to the town's mileage. The farmers enjoyed the chance to visit together. The well-trained horses would follow if their driver climbed onto the cart ahead. There was the welcome noon interval in the warm sun, while horses ate their oats and hay, and men opened baskets and pails of hearty food. Many a farm lad of twelve or fourteen earned his first real cash shoveling at the bank or helping spread on the road. Working out the taxes was not only an important matter of economics, but also an enjoyable and anticipated time of the farm year's calendar.

OLD SOOT-COVERED KETTLES ARE STILL IN USE ON MANY farms. They are not so common today as they were a generation ago, when almost every farm had its kettle for boiling the small potatoes for the pigs. Or, perhaps, the farmer had a favorite formula for combining cooked corn meal, turnips, and carrots for those last few weeks before butchering time.

In days long ago there were outdoor kettles for soap-making, clothes washing, hog swill, and apple butter. At the turn of the century, especially in the Northeast, two of the black containers were commonly used. There was, first, the giant of the family—the big kettle that heated the water for scalding the hogs in butchering season. Sometimes it was out of doors; sometimes it was built into a brick arch in the room between kitchen and woodshed. This big kettle had other uses. It could be used for boiling down extra sap in sugar-making time; it helped a man steam oak planks and timbers if he needed a new stoneboat or a runner for his traverse.

But the kettle that many a man recalls most vividly was the one that hung in the back yard. The setup was simple: two posts six or eight feet apart, a sturdy timber resting on the posts, a chain with a hook hanging from the middle of the timber and the kettle handle resting in the chain hook. Each afternoon, when the shadows began to creep across the mowing in late autumn, it was a farm lad's chore to start a fire beneath the soot-encrusted pot and boil the potatoes, corn, and other ingredients that made a tempting, nutritious pail of hog swill.

Homely, simple, and efficient, the iron kettles have played their part well. Today one often sees a kettle on a front lawn, filled with petunias or geraniums. The era of black pots is ending, but they will remain in memory for a long time to come.

S URELY WE CANNOT EVER BE EXPECTED TO GO FAR INTO
the autumn without having some authentic prophe-
cies of the winter. Usually, fairly early the men who read the
signs are ready with definite prognostications. It is one of
the things we have come to depend upon. Weather prophets
are not retiring personalities; they may be wrong, for weather
has traits of rugged individualism. Nevertheless, each fall we
expect to read what these authorities foresee. The fact that
one school sees a mild, open winter, while another predicts
a plethora of blizzards and zero spells need cast no shadow
on the enjoyment.

Of course, one can qualify with a little study. Take the
simple weathervane of the thickness of the fur on gray
squirrels' tails. A bushy tail can mean a hard winter; or, if
you prefer, it can also mean a light one. The reasoning in the
latter instance is that the winter will be so easy that Kaolah
will spend much time out of doors and wants his caudal ap-
pendage well protected.

The experts become engrossed in studying the cattails and
the dogwood buds; scanning the moss on the north side of
hemlocks and spruces; watching the chipmunks and the red
squirrels. Have the woodchucks gone to bed early? Isn't some
hardy northwoodsman ready with a report on whether his
whiskers are curling unduly on these crisp fall mornings?

Meanwhile, time is flying. The autumn moon will soon be
here. The Milky Way makes a pearly path through the
myriad stars. Nights are still and frosty and crisp. The corn
shocks stand stacked in the fields, and pumpkins are piled in
the farmyard. Come, come, weather prophets! We are await-
ing your verdicts.

*W*HEN AUTUMN WINDS AND LASHING RAINS HAVE beaten the leaves from maples, birches, elms, and beeches, when the thick mat of grass in the meadow and the thin carpeting of the upland pasture are crinkled by black frosts, there remain banners of red to accentuate the browns and grays and tans of the countryside.

The velvet, or staghorn, sumac lifts its scarlet foliage and deep-red conical clusters of fuzz-covered berries long after the leaves of other trees have become a sodden blanket on the woodland floor. The oaks cling to their leaves through the winter, but these turn dull brown and grayish black. The sumacs' brilliant, wine-colored leaves, with their delicate, closely spaced veins, are a fitting background for the gorgeously colored clusters of berries.

In early summer, the dense panicles of flowers appear on the ends of short branches. The staghorn's pollen-bearing and seed-bearing blossoms blend with the long, graceful, compound leaves. Country boys like to feel the dense growth of velvety hairs on the soft, smooth back of the young branches.

Autumn, however, is the season for appreciating the beauty of the sumac, as it lifts its plump, pointed banners in massed effect in pasture corners, along country roads, and by the stone walls that bound meadows and mowing fields. When the leaves fall, the small red banners cling tight to the ends of the short branches. Through the gray days of early winter they hold their color. The birds feast on the small, brown berries inside the fuzz, and the deer come out of the swamps to eat the hard-shelled nutlets. Even when the snow lies deep over the northland, the red banners remain—a splash of color on the painting of winter.

*I*N THE LATE AUTUMN THEY LIE EXPOSED, OPEN BOOKS of the past. One finds them beside the back-country roads, on boulder-strewn hillsides beside faint traces of a long-abandoned road, and on the ledgy brows of low mountains. Over the granite stones is a tangle of wild briers; the canes form an intricate etching against the weather-grayed, lichen-covered rocks. In one corner of the cellar may be a few sumacs, with their branches of garnet berries, or a group of gray birches reaching slender fingers to the sky. The dooryard that once echoed to the shouts of playing children is a tangle of alders, wild cherries, and pines. In the midst of the natural wilderness the cellar hole remains, a reminder of the days before the fertile, level lands of the West beckoned to the new frontier.

A century ago, this place was a thriving farm. Here on the hillside, facing the south and overlooking a valley, a young farmer and his bride built themselves a home place. This cellar hole was part of that home. In it were stored the results of the family's labor. Above it was the large kitchen, where a man and his family were safe when winter storms howled around the corners. On one side of the fireplace a mother sewed while her children stretched on the floor and read books and dreamed the dreams of youth. On the other side, a man with steady eyes and work-hardened hands read his Bible and the weekly paper.

December is a good month to see the old cellar holes. On a quiet, sunny day they lie revealed—a reminder of the past. They are monuments to a nation's development. From these homes came men and women who helped to push a new nation across prairies and mountains. Covered with brambles and bushes, often with a lilac clump still standing beside a granite doorstep, the cellar holes are a part of our history.

A HISTORY OF MAN COULD BE WRITTEN IN TERMS OF HIS ability to provide himself light. No chapter in that history would be more revealing than the story of the service of the humble kerosene lantern. Down through long centuries, man has used a lantern of some sort. We do not know when he first realized that he could submerge part of a wick in animal oil and obtain light from the other end; but, when kerosene came into his service, he soon contrived to imprison the wick in a globe, so that the lantern could be carried. To kerosene, or coal oil, as it is still called in certain areas, we owe much. Uncounted millions of railroad lanterns, with double-wire protection around the heavy globe, have followed the railroads as they pushed over mountains and plains toward the land of the setting sun.

Kerosene lanterns have hung beneath farm wagons on the way to town each Saturday night; they have served their turn on the sides of gay carriages and sleighs when city folk drove about the streets in early evening. They have hung as signals on ships and, today, stand or hang in sentried rows when a street or a road is under repair. They have served for light in man-made caverns deep in the earth. Not so very long ago, the lamplighter made his daily round along the street, lighting the lamps inside the wrought-iron lanterns that stood on oaken posts.

No one can tell what the sight of a lantern has meant in terms of human happiness. On many a lonely road, in many an isolated home, the sight of a gleaming lantern has given comforting heart glow—relief from solitude. It is symbolical that once upon a time the light of two lanterns gleamed from a church steeple and a man sped off to awaken a new country to its destiny. Lanterns are good companions. Giving light to dark places, bringing cheer to human hearts, they help man's feet keep the path that leads upward.

M ANY MEN NOW WORKING IN OFFICES AND FACTORIES can remember when October was apple-butter time. Probably, the capacious copper kettles are still to be found on many farms. The antique collectors cannot have found them all. Farmers' wives can get the ingredients—sweet cider and apples, with a bit of sassafras root for that pungent, unique, sweet-sour flavor.

Making apple butter is an all-day and part of the evening process. Frequently, the twenty- or thirty-gallon kettle was out of doors; sometimes, it was in a specially built arch in the woodshed or the summer kitchen. A recipe might say: "Take thirty gallons of sweet cider; boil down a half; add four twelve-quart pails of apples previously peeled and quartered, with cores removed."

That, however, is the mere mechanics of a delicate process. A farm wife who had gained fame for her apple butter could no more describe the subtle and intangible aspects of its deliciousness than can the cook who makes a superlative Indian pudding. Who except those with a sixth sense can distinguish between a simmer and a light boiling? How does one tell when the cider is condensed exactly enough to receive its apples? Who can describe to another exactly what is meant by slow stirring as the bubbling, spicy, nostril-tickling mass approaches the final stage?

Those are the problems of the process. The important thing is that apple butter is being made. The steady fire of dried oak and maple chunks burns through the hours; the magic of heat changes cider and apples to a rich, brownish-red paste. On a cold, blizzardy evening in January, when the countryman spreads its tangy goodness on a fresh biscuit for supper, he knows that he'll be glad to cut an extra bit of firewood for apple-butter time, next fall.

*W*HEN OCTOBER'S FLAMING COLORS HAVE GIVEN WAY
to November's browns, when the harvest is safely
under cover in barn and crib, and when the parlor stove has
been set again on its square of zinc in the living room, then
the time has come to bank the house against the cold and
winds of winter.

There are, one cheerfully admits, diverse opinions on the
subject. One school holds that closely packed hemlock
branches will repel King Winter's offensives; the eclectic
group of philosophers is likely to insist that a strip of building
paper held in place with small, nailed bits of wood serves the
purpose. There is merit in both. But traditional, time-proved
house banking goes beyond this.

First, the peeled oak stakes and the long sixteen-inch-wide
white-pine boards are taken from their summer storage space
on the scaffold over the end mow in the barn. The stakes are
driven into the ground about a foot from the foundation, and
at ten-foot intervals around the house. The boards are then
set in place against them. As the countryman makes his
trough around the house, he thinks of the winter, years ago,
when he felled a few of the beautiful, tall pines in the back
lot just for this purpose. Banking boards are vital equipment
in the north country.

At the mill the wagon is filled with the tan-gold, pungent
sawdust. The resinous, acrid, tangy aroma seems to blend
with the season's mood. Back at the farm the trough is filled,
tamped down, and filled some more, until it is level full of
efficient insulation—sixteen inches high and a foot wide.

That night, as he comes in from milking, the farmer stops
a moment and lets the lantern's light play over the band of
protection around the house. As he goes in to supper, there's
contentment in his face. The house is banked for winter.

F. W. Went

M ANY WRITERS HAVE PAID THEIR RESPECTS TO HER, and perhaps none more happily than Coleridge when he said, "Most beautiful of forest trees, The Lady of the Woods." The white birch has feminine grace and beauty; she adorns the spot, wherever she may be growing. Calm, symmetrical, slender, the tree fits into any environment. Maples, oaks, and beeches dominate their surroundings by sheer, massive, masculine aggressiveness. The white birches also dominate, but with the subtle strength of the aristocrats of yesteryear.

The Lady of the Woods is perhaps the best-known native tree. It is closely associated with our history and literature. Every American child knows that its bark was used to build the canoes of the Red Men and the early explorers in this wilderness land. Alas! school children and some beyond school age have ruthlessly torn off The Lady's almost transparent layers of thin, pliable bark.

The white birch is not so widespread as its cousin, the gray. But in northern New England and northern New York it thrives well in the hot summers and zeroish winters. He who has seen a northern river rushing between ranks of the beau-tiful trees or a small north-country pond surrounded by them, has seen one of nature's loveliest pictures. A family of white birches against a background of spruces, hemlocks, or pines is a cherished picture on many an upland farm.

The white birch wins its way by gentleness. The lashing winds of late autumn whip it close to earth; but, when the storm has passed, it stands again in quiet dignity. Snow and sleet may bow its patrician grace; but, when the sun unlocks the frozen weight, The Lady rises, unflurried and serene. In her beautiful white robes she reigns in her kingdom, always gracious and lovely, always calm and friendly.

*L*ATE IN THE FALL, WHEN BARNS AND CRIBS ARE stuffed with food for the livestock and the house cellar is full of good things for the family, when everything is snugly banked for the winter, and the icehouse is cleaned out and ready for the midwinter harvest, many a farmer decides to dig a new well.

The dowsing, or divining, rod has been a subject of controversy for many centuries. It is surrounded with superstition and folklore. The professional dowser has his vehement defenders and his articulate scoffers. In most rural communities there is one person who has a reputation as a "waterfinder." Many farmers who pretend to laugh at the divining rod make a dicker with the dowser—and agree to pay if water be found.

The divining rod was so well known in the fifteenth and sixteenth centuries that writers commented upon it. In the same century that saw the *Pinta*, the *Niña*, and the *Santa Maria* cross the Atlantic, miners were using the dowsing rod to locate certain minerals in various localities in Europe. Scientists have studied the phenomenon, and at least one has publicly said that the rod bends downward "without voluntary deception on the part of the dowser."

Anyone who has observed the process knows its fascination. One may scoff; but he must wonder. To watch a man walk back and forth over the ground and then to see the forked branch of witch hazel, willow, apple, or beech turn irresistibly downward is to glimpse a bit of the supernatural —if one believes in dowsing. According to the Encyclopaedia Britannica, "the best dowsers have generally been more or less illiterate men engaged in some humble occupation." Perhaps men in "humble" occupations are closer to the spirit of Mother Earth. At any rate, the dowser helps to find water for man and his animals. Whether we believe in his powers or not, he is part of our rural folklore.

*I*T IS DIFFICULT TO DECIDE WHETHER CROWS LEARNED how to conduct a convention from watching the procedures of major political parties or whether, in olden days, political leaders watched crows in session and decided to pattern their meetings on this model.

A crow convention follows all the accepted rules. As they begin to gather in the clump of elms in the meadow, there is a period of preliminary speechmaking, confusion, and noise. Favorite sons make raucous caucus with minority groups of delegates. There is flitting back and forth from one camp to another by professionals, who seek to balance group against group. There is trading and jockeying for position. Small bands fly from headquarters in the tree hotels to spots on the ground, talk secretly together, and then rejoin the main group.

There are constant shifts, in the preliminary stages. There are moments of sudden surprise when a rumor of major import catches all off guard. A short period of silence is followed by an outburst of louder noise. Little by little the tension mounts. Messengers come and go. Delegates form groups and wheel through the air in demonstration of the strength of their candidates. At length, when the noise and confusion are at their height, one senses the approaching climax.

Suddenly, the screaming, shouting, and confusion subside. One voice, lone and authoritative, caws forth a series of dogmatic commands. The leader is elected and the platform for the season is announced. By twos and threes and fours the delegates disperse and fly to the woodlands. When the crows finish their convention, the tumult and the shouting are over. That's a salubrious feature of crow politics.

NOVEMBER IS A HALFWAY MONTH, HALFWAY BE-
tween fall and winter; halfway between the reds
and golds of October and the grays of December. In the
Northland, the earth lies cold and shivering, waiting for the
snow to blanket its bareness. Not that November is a dreary
month. There are, to be sure, days when low-hanging nimbus
clouds spit sleet and rain; but there are also days when the
sky is blue and cumulus clouds move slowly along like Gar-
gantuan submarines of the sky lanes—days when the light is
peculiarly clear and the bark patterns of the trees stand forth
in bold relief.

It is the month of browns. In the meadows, upland mowing fields, and mountain pastures, the frost-tinged grasses are
a light, soft brown color. Along city streets and wall-lined
country roads there are drifts of brown leaves, heaped in piles
in corners, swished together in corners. They are beneath the
trimmed hedges of the suburbs and tucked among the
sumacs, gray birches, and alders of rural lanes. Along the
fence rows the dry, crisp stalks of goldenrod rustle in the
nippy air, and in the swamps the cattails lift brown banners
to November's sky.

Brown banners wave high in the air. The oak trees cling
to their leaves until well into the winter or even on into the
spring. In November the leaves may be a rich, deep, winy
brown, smooth and silky to the touch, and the veins clear as
the lines on a simple, uncrowded etching. Later, when storms
and cold have swirled and bitten, the leaves gradually lose
their depth of color and change to the faded browns we see
in midwinter; but while it's still November, the symphony of
browns is at the climax. This is not a bad season of the year,
between autumn and winter.

IT IS BEAN-THRESHING TIME ON THE FARM. ON A CLEAR, windy day—usually a Saturday, when the boys are home to help—the barn doors are opened and the floor is swept. The red kidneys, or the yellow eyes, or the white pea beans are pulled from the branch-stubbed poles around which they were stacked to dry, and are spread in a six- or eight-inch layer on the floor.

The flails are taken from the spikes where they hang during the year. Flails are used to "thresh out" the beans from their tough, wizened, brittle pods. Flailing is an art. There are those who achieve smooth rhythm and efficient results; others no more than master the rudiments.

The handle is four or five feet long. The beating stick is two or three feet long and is fastened to the handle with a stout cord or a leather thong. The whole flail is lifted in the air and brought forward so that the beating stick strikes on an even keel. Many a lad learning to thresh beans has received a smart tap on the back of his head when he brought the handle too high. Each horizontal blow shatters dry pods and the beans spill out.

Over and over the surface go the flails. Beans pop into the air. After a time, the whole mass is stirred with pitchforks and flailed again. At length come the welcome words: "All right, boys, pitch off the pods and we'll winnow 'em."

The beans, debris, and dust are swept and shoveled into a big pile. A basketful is taken outside where the wind is strong. Then the beans are poured back and forth from one basket to another until the wind has taken all the dirt away. When the beans are winnowed and stored in the big wooden buckets in the back kitchen, Father makes his expected remark: "Well, boys, there are our Saturday-night suppers for another year."

Beef Stew

*P*HILOSOPHERS HAVE LONG PONDERED THE PROBLEM OF rise and fall among nations. Ingenious and logical hypotheses have been promulgated. There are those who believe that a nation's eating habits and its position among its peers have a direct correlation. We view with perturbation the decline of beef stew.

We do not refer to quantity. A dish allegedly beef stew is commonly offered on menus. A concoction with that label is tossed together in many a home. It is the quality that needs attention. Beef stew, humble and plebeian by reputation, can be one of life's gastronomical experiences. But it isn't a dish to be mixed in casual nonchalance.

First of all, one's attitude must be right. The making of a beef stew should be approached in a leisurely manner and with full concentration. If one is disquieted about the stock market, if he's wondering whether he should be putting on the storm windows or paying the month's bills, he cannot receive all that beef stew has to offer.

A proper stew should always be made in the morning. After the chunks of beef are half cooked, the vegetables should be added and cooked right in the beef-flavored water. It is rankest heresy to cook the vegetables separately. A stew should contain white potatoes, carrots, onions, turnips, just a bit of cabbage, and plenty of sweet potatoes. It's unthinkable to rate a beef stew triple-A priority that doesn't include sweet potatoes. After the stew is cooked, it should be set aside to cool. It is the reheating that brings out all the subtle nuances, the utterly delicious and the completely satisfying flavor. There's no proof that Jupiter served beef stew at the Olympian meals; but, if he had known about it, ambrosia would not have received so much publicity.

*T*HE COUNTRYMAN KNOWS WINTER IS SHARPENING HIS knife when the neighborly, hustling, black-capped chickadees begin to appear in the old apple trees behind the barn. There's something heart-warming and appealing about the little fellows as they scramble around the trunks and limbs, poking into crevices of the weather-frayed bark. Miniature acrobats of the winter bird world, they maneuver with equal ease in any position.

Part of their appeal is due to their unquenchable optimism. It makes little difference to them whether it's a day dominated by November's browns, December's grays, or ten below zero on a January morning when all the landscape is brittle white. The blackcap takes the weather in stride. His cheery, altoish "Chick-a-dee-dee" heartens the farmer as he comes in from the morning's milking.

During the summer, the chickadee and his mate have been busy raising one or two broods hatched from tiny, white eggs specked with reddish brown. Their favorite nesting place is a hollow stub, especially an old birch trunk. But now, when winter's poised for his southward trek, the blackcaps like to come around the buildings; and, when a man's out in the wood lot chopping next season's fuel supply, the chickadees seem to gather round. When the chips are flying and the tangy aroma of fresh-cut wood fills the air, it's good to hear the little fellows chant their throaty theme, "Chick-a-dee-dee-dee, chick-a-dee-dee-dee."

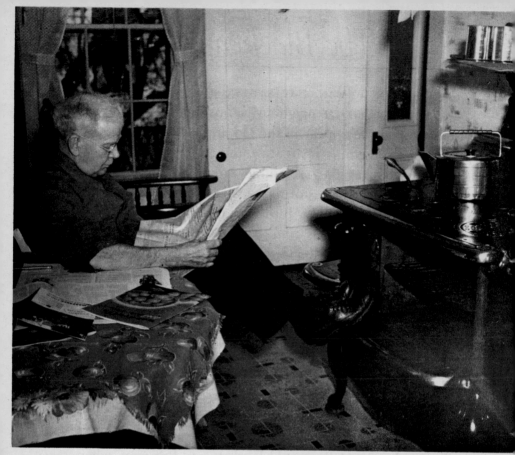

F. W. Went

*P*OEMS HAVE BEEN WRITTEN AND PAEANS SUNG TO THE nickel-plated, aristocratic base-burner, but too little has been said and too few verses have been dedicated to the humble kitchen stove. Gas and electric stoves are modernistically efficient. They serve their purpose well, and doubtless in the Elysian days of postwar marvels they will increase in numbers. But they do not have the cheery comfortableness of the wood- or coal-burning range.

There are logical reasons for this. Who ever heard of a man's coming home from a hard day's work and putting his stockinged feet in the oven of a gas stove? But on many a farm where kitchen and dining room are combined, the countryman prefers to spend the evenings in front of the friendly kitchen stove instead of going into the living room. Feet that have been close to snow all day in the wood lot delight in the toasting warmth of the capacious oven.

The copper teakettle sings on the back of the stove. Shep is curled on the floor behind it, making little eager moans as he dreams of the big woodchuck in the pasture wall. Puss purrs on the old sofa by the window. The heart of a kitchen is the stove—solid, big, gleamingly clean, it dominates the room. Coal may be best for steady heat and it ensures a warm room on a zero morning; but there are those who cherish a wood fire and delight in a wood box filled with pieces of solid oak, maple, and ash. With either fuel, the kitchen stove is equally cooperative. On literally millions of farms and in many village homes the kitchen stove plays its important role with warm dependability.

$\mathcal{J}$T IS HIGH TIME SOMETHING WAS DONE ABOUT WRISTERS.
A news item remarked recently that in the marvelous
postwar era we shall have light winter clothing—clothing even
lighter in weight than that now used in summer. One cannot
be dogmatic. Science is awesome in its ability to provide
needed items to meet specific objectives. A world that can
produce B-29's and dehydrated, mild-aromaed garlic can
eventually overcome tight collars around men's necks and
tight belts around their midriffs.

However, in the present stage of clothing styles, the wrister
has been sadly neglected since the first decade of the century. It is mildly disappointing that Mr. Webster does not
recognize the word "wrister." Noah calls it "wristlet." His
succinct definition is acceptable to the countryman: "a band
worn around the wrist, as for protection or ornament."

There are those today, especially grandmothers, who
claim that people do not dress adequately for the months of
long nights. They insist that long ones, rubbers, warm gloves,
and wristers are a natural concomitant of the season. A generation ago, the wrister problem was a daily issue. In the eyes
of their elders, the young folks were lacking in judgment
and discretion if they ventured forth without their wristers.
The fact that elders always feel that way about the succeed-
ing generation has, of course, nothing to do with the problem.
The wrister was an essential part of what an adequately
clothed person should wear. That two- or three-inch band
of warm, knitted material was a buffer against dangerous
elements. Sometimes a farm lad felt that Grandmother's in-
sistence was related to the fact that she delighted in knitting
the things in gay and colorful combinations of green, red,
blue, and brown.

DECEMBER IS LOW TWELVE OF NATURE'S DAY. NO HOPE now of a period of Indian summer. From now on it's simply an occasional spell of warmer weather. The venerable turnkey, Winter, has inserted his implement in the padlock and snapped the combination. Snow covers the Northland; the woodchucks, bears, turtles, frogs, and toads are dug in for the long siege.

There's beauty, however, in the gray days of December. The stratus and nimbus clouds are suspended low above meadows, fields, and upland pastures. Of all the months, it's the most peaceful and quiet. The blanket of snow hushes one's footfalls as he tramps over fields and through woods. The stone walls are capped with whiteness and the craggy ledges and granite boulders of the sidehills wear white caps. The weeds in the garden, the stalks of goldenrod in the corners, the jaunty cattails in the swamps, and the grasses that show above the snow have turned from their autumn tans and browns to the grayish shades they will wear for the next months. The weathered, splintery posts at the pasture barway and the peeled maple-sapling bars seem to wear a richer sheen of silvery gray against the whiteness that covers the land.

December is a gray month, but there's no lack of activity. The pheasants come into the garden to search for weed seeds; the white-tailed deer come up from the swamps to paw the snow beneath the Baldwin and greening trees for frozen fruit. And when the farmer takes his axe to the wood lot and begins to get up next season's woodpile, the chickadees, nuthatches, and downies come around to enjoy his company. December is quiet and gray, but it's a soft, relaxing gray. Night falls early in the gray month, but the countryman looks forward to the long evenings. With a crackling fire in the stove, a dish of juicy apples and a favorite farm paper, the gray month has compensations.

EDDY HAS A SHADY REPUTATION AMONG FARMERS AND farm boys. The countryman claims the red fox is too fond of broilers, fryers, and roasters; his son tries to trap Reddy for the valuable pelt. But Vulpes fulva is fully capable of looking after himself. He's one of the original wild folk that have held their own as farms, towns, and villages have been carved from the woodlands.

Reddy is an odd mixture of philosopher, playboy, and man of action. He delights in leading the hounds a merry chase on brisk, sunny December days. He stalks his game with infinite patience; but when a rabbit or a mouse escapes his leap, there's no bemoaning the ill luck. He simply trots off purposefully and unhurriedly to another hunting ground, ears up and brush lifted.

Those who have had the opportunity to study Reddy through field glasses are often surprised by his similarity to a small dog. He has a black stub of a nose, large bright eyes, big ears, and a long, bushy tail. In the spring, Reddy enjoys a romp with his children in the open area before the den. The baby foxes tumble and wrestle with each other in helter-skelter fashion—for all the world like a litter of collie puppies.

He has a cosmopolitan appetite. Chicken is only occasionally on the menu. In winter, he eats what he can get—rabbits, mice, grouse, frozen apples, dried berries. In spring and summer he enjoys a turtle and turtle eggs, snakes, a few broilers if the chicken fence is vulnerable, and a bit of fresh fruit, such as wild raspberries and blackberries. Rufus, the Red, is shrewd and playful; but he asks no odds and adapts himself to modern conditions. The countryman, as he sees Reddy trot across the snow-covered upper mowing field on a December day, smiles a bit ruefully, remembering last spring's experience. But it wouldn't be natural if no red foxes were around to add spice to country living.

Baked Beans

$\mathcal{J}$T OUGHT TO BE UNDERSTOOD THAT THE SUBJECT OF baked beans is not one for unanimity of opinion. Down East in Maine, they favor a medium-sized onion in each pot. Vermonters snort at such heretical goings-on and use a little maple syrup instead of molasses as sweetening. Both Maine and Vermont outwardly agree that brown bread plentifully studded with raisins is the natural complement of a plate of beans. New Hampshiremen insist that the way to eat beans is: first, place a slice of well-buttered, crisp-crusted, freshly baked, homemade, white bread on the plate; second, cover this slice of buttered bread with lots of juicy beans and pork; third, repeat the entire process.

Even within a single state there are schisms. There are those who insist on a sprinkling of sugar on the heaped plateful; while others use a few beans as a minor partner to huge amounts of chili sauce, chutney, piccalilli, sweet tomato pickle, sweet cucumber pickle, pickled pears, spiced crab apples, or pickled watermelon rind. There are men of experience and judgment who place a piece of butter in the center of each heaping plateful. The golden rivulets wind their way among the mealy nuggets and blend with the rich juice from the baking.

As one would expect in a democracy, opinions differ about the merits of varieties. There are those who claim the finest eating is with yellow eyes; others prefer red kidneys; some are for white peas; and a few know the tasty succulence of Jacob's cattle beans. The countryman is broad-minded about the problem. All he asks is that the beans shall be soaked Friday night, cooked all day Saturday, that they contain molasses, mustard, salt, a good-sized piece of salt pork that has both fat and lean, a small onion, and plenty of juice. There is one other essential. There must be enough left over for Sunday morning breakfast.

F. W. We

*H*ALF A CENTURY AND MORE AGO, BEFORE THIN SOIL and rocky terrain surrendered to the fertile lands of river vallëys west of the Appalachians, farms long since abandoned to the woods and summer people commonly had their orchards. Now these are surrounded by woods; among the apple trees are gray birches, alders, and a tangle of brush.

The old trees are gaunt and twisted. The limbs of the Baldwins, greenings, and snow apples tend to grow high into the air. In the decaying trunks and main limbs flickers, chickadees, and bluebirds build their nests. Bare, dead limbs may be ringed with riveted, circular holes where the redheaded woodpecker has dug for larvae and grubs.

Perhaps there is a frost-shaken stone wall about. A century ago, a farmer and his sons with a pair of oxen and a stoneboat hauled these rocks from the mowing field and built this wall around slender shoots, which grew into these aged trees. Today the weathered gray wall is covered with wild vines and seems an integral part of the picture.

In December and early January, before the snow blanket grows too deep, an abandoned orchard is a favorite rendezvous of wild life. The white-tailed deer comes in the hesitant dawn to paw the snow and search for the frozen nubbins of fruit. The partridge walks among the leaves and light snow and tears the soggy, punky flesh, to get the seeds in the core. Here one finds, too, the tiny, dainty tracks of the wood mouse that came hunting for a seed overlooked by the partridge.

The old apple trees, gnarled, storm-torn, and neglected, have stood stanchly through the years. They have known heat and blizzard, rain and snow. Slowly and inevitably they must succumb to the law of nature. Meanwhile, they serve out their time faithfully and well. Abandoned by man, they have become a part of nature's scheme.

*T*IME WAS WHEN THE BLACKSMITH SHOP WAS A THRILL-
ing and wonderful place to a farm lad who drove the
team to town on a rainy day for a new set all around. The
grimy, dirt-streaked windows were covered with a tangled
mass of sooty cobwebs. In one corner was a high heap of old
horseshoes of all sizes and weights; in another was a laby-
rinthine mass of wheels, cultivators, plow points, and odds
and ends of metal. The floor was dark and rough and dirty,
with real dirt—the accumulation of years. From the blackened
timbers overhead hung hundreds of horseshoes—dainty lightweight ones for Deacon Jones's bay pacer: thick, heavy ones
for the plodding draft horses.

The smith himself was a picturesque character in his tat-
tered leather apron. It was fascinating to see him pump the
bellows with one hand and poke the coal around the heating
shoe with the other. When the shoe was red-hot, he snatched
it from the fire with tongs and laid it on the anvil. Myriad
red sparks flew in all directions as he beat the shoe into
shape. Then it was plunged into the wooden half-tub of dark-
colored, brackish water. Clouds of gray-streaked steam rolled
upward to the rafters. Deftly the smith lifted a leg of phleg-
matic old Jerry and laid the shoe against the hoof. The acrid,
pungent smell of singed hoof pervaded the shop. The nails
were driven with firm, decisive strokes. A coarse file
smoothed down the edges of the hoof. The leg dropped with
a thump.

It is good to know that the sparks are flying again. With
horse power growing more important and the necessity of
making farm equipment stretch through at least another
season, the blacksmith shops in town and village will resound
to anvil blows for some time to come.

F. W. Wen

*T*HERE WAS A TIME, NOT SO LONG AGO, WHEN IT WAS AN axiom of the countryside that you could judge a farmer by his woodpile. A good farmer took pride in his fuel supply. In the winter or the early spring it was sawed, split, and stacked in the woodshed.

On frosty, star-studded nights when the cold air hangs like a blanket over hills and valleys, waiting to tuck the earth in for its long, strength-restoring sleep, many a farmer pauses as he comes from the barn. The yellow light of the lantern makes a picture as it plays over the stacked tiers.

A real country woodshed is a place of deep, fundamental satisfaction. It represents honest labor—the cutting, the trimming and hauling; the sawing, as the whirring knife-edged teeth sang through the oak, maple, beech, and hickory; the splitting, as the axe flashed down and hit the exact spot so that a chunk separated along the grain; the stacking, as the symmetrical tiers rose toward the woodshed attic floor.

It's a place of good smells. A woodshed that has been used for years has a tangy, pungent aroma. There's the resinous zip of the pine limbs, which make a quick kindling on zero winter mornings when the hoarfrost is deep on kitchen windows; the nostril-tickling acridness of red oak; the zesty tang of old apple wood; the bland smoothness of sugar maple and beech; the peculiarly pungent odor of hemlock; and the clean, exhilarating smell of cedar. Penetrating through all the other smells is that dry, slightly musty aroma of the inches-deep base of splinters, bits of bark, and debris that is the accumulation of years.

Woodsheds are part of America, the same as johnnycake, two-seated democrats, buck saws, and pancakes and maple syrup.

*T*HE PARLOR STOVE—BASE-BURNER, SOME PREFER TO call it—is part of the history of America. Boys and girls have gazed through the mica square in the stove door and dreamed youth's dreams as they watched the flames curl from the chunks of maple, oak, and hickory.

In many farm homes today, setting up the parlor stove in the fall and removing it to the back kitchen or the woodshed in the spring are regular semiannual tasks. The countryman has special hardwood rollers on which to push it back and forth. In the living room, it sits on a square of zinc, placed reasonably far from the wall—not so much, one might think, to heat the whole room as to give opportunity to all members of the family to sit around it. For a stove is merely a caged fire, and who likes to sit far from the hearth?

In winter, second only to the kitchen range, the parlor stove is the heart of family life. Tall, spacious, and sturdy, it defies the elements. Its black surfaces polished to a gleaming luster, its nickel scrollwork shining like silver, and its ornamental top pointing heavenward, it serves its purpose well. Those words sometimes seen on the nickel-plated footrest— "Home Comfort"—were literally and spiritually true. It may be, as scientists predict, that sometime in the future all homes will be comfortable because the sun's rays will be canned in summer for winter use; but the friendly parlor stove will always have a share in our tradition.

Chopping Wood

CERTAIN TOOLS HAVE ALWAYS ACCOMPANIED MAN SINCE he made the epochal discovery that metals could be fused and wrought into useful implements. The axe is a tool that has hewn history. Many men, today, in the country and in the city, delight in the "feel" of a good axe.

There's more in chopping wood than the cutting down of trees. That's a part of it. The axe is intimately associated with our nation's history. It was only a short time ago, historically, that a man was equipped to carve his home from the frontier wilderness if he had an axe, a rifle, and a hoe.

When one goes into the wood lot on a winter's day, he feels a kinship with the calm spirit of nature. Here among trees that have seen the miracle of spring, the fruition of harvest, and the blizzards of winter for a century or more, the ills and cares that infest man-made society fall into proper perspective. Pines, hemlocks, and firs murmur among themselves: beeches, maples, and oaks are traced against the winter sky like dry-point etchings. Chickadees chant their roundelays; rabbits hop from one brush heap to another; partridges whir up with startling suddenness.

The countryman will chop wood. He'll select his trees with care; he'll enjoy swinging the sharp-bladed axe. Thick chips will fly and the pleasant, pungent aroma of fresh wood will scent the air. But when day is done and he walks down the pasture slope toward the lights in the farmhouse windows, a man who has been chopping knows that he has increased his wealth by more than a pile of logs in the wood lot.

*T*HE HEART OF WINTER IS THE TIME OF BELLS. THE AGE of cars and trucks, robots and flying battleships is not one of musical sounds; but before civilization grew so complicated, wintertime was bell time.

A farmer had his own ideas about it. There were bells of many sizes, worn in various ways on the horse or the equipment. One countryman preferred big three-inch bells on a broad leather strap encircling the horse's belly. Another liked short strings of smaller bells, fastened to the shafts of sleighs, cutters, and pungs. Often each string had bells of varying sizes and almost played a tune as the roadster whisked briskly toward church, grange, or Saturday-evening trading at the general store.

No less individual were the single bells that hung from the collars of work teams. Some men preferred big, rectangular bells with a clanking baritone note; others liked good-sized brass replicas of the cast-iron bell in the church belfry; and still others, smaller bells, which gave high-pitched, sweet tones. At the turn of the century, when farmers went to town with the two-horse sled or the one-horse bob, everyone knew which neighbor was coming by the sound of the bells.

Somehow, the chimes fitted the scene. When fields, meadows, and upland pastures were white, and pearl-gray smoke spiraled from farm chimneys, it was good to hear the musical chimes over the valley as a snappy Morgan headed for town. When a neighbor went by with a load of logs for Johnson's mill, the bells on the collars sounded a rhythmic, marking-time tempo, while the hoofs and sled runners made squeaking, crunching sounds in packed tracks. Perhaps acoustics are better in winter; perhaps there are fewer sounds in nature to distract. The bells in winter made welcome music.

Snow Rolling

*W*HEN A SNOWSTORM STARTS TODAY, THE COUNTER-
offensive opens as soon as the Weather Man gives
the nod. A generation ago, before horse and ox power had
given way to that of petroleum, a bad storm blew itself out
before the roads were broken.

Then, after the morning chores were done and paths were
shoveled to mailbox, hen house, and horse barn, the farmer
and his boys hitched up the span of Morgan mares and joined
forces with a neighbor and his team on the snow roller. After
a howling northeaster, three or four teams were sometimes
needed. Heavy and solidly built, it resembled two barrels
made of staves, with open spaces between the longitudinally
nailed bars. With an ingenious front hitch, the connected
rollers would handle snow of varying depths where drifts
blocked the road. The purpose was to roll down the snow so
that families with sleds, pungs, or sleighs could get to town.
Each successive storm layer was rolled. When the warm
winds of March began to unlock the frozen world, the packed
snow of the roads lasted longer than the snow in fields and
meadows.

Snow rolling gave a day or two of happy excitement, and
a lad was glad to earn a dollar a day—a man's pay. In an
emergency, a teen-ager could do almost a man's work, and
emergency work pays high wages. It was fun to cling to the
framework of the roller as the horses plunged forward. To sit
in the driver's seat high in air and handle the reins was a
great honor. Not that the horses needed much help; they had
pulled the roller many times. It was fun even to join the
crowd and shovel through the packed drifts that gathered in
the same places, winter after winter. In "hard" winters the
cuts through bad spots became tunnels. Snow-rolling days
are past; but many a man in a city office, looking out at falling
snowflakes, recalls the time when he was part of a shouting,
jolly crew rolling the roads after a winter's storm.

OR THE BENEFIT OF URBANITES WHOSE EDUCATION does not include country living a generation ago, it should be stated that a pung is not a sleigh. A sleigh, with either one or two seats, has a high dashboard, and the seats have high backs. A pung has a low dashboard, the backs of the seats are low, and the seats are removable. The pung was a utility affair. It carried the family to church and grange meetings; with eggs and butter packed under the seat, the whole family rode in it to town on Saturday evening in winter to do the trading.

With the rear seat removed, there was ample room for a jug or two of cream. On many farms, it was a lad's job to take the cream to the creamery on a Saturday morning in winter and to bring home a bag or two of meal for the stock. With a snappy roadster between the offset shafts (the reason for only two tracks on country roads in the winter), it was fun to head for town. Sleigh bells jingled; white clouds came back from the mare's nostrils; the steel runners slid over the hard-packed tracks with thin, high-pitched squeaks. The horse's hoofs beat a crunchy, dry-sounding tattoo on the cold snow.

Though the pung was a utilitarian vehicle, many a farmer enjoyed trimming it up a bit. On a rainy fall day, a man could indulge his imagination and creative impulses with paints and brushes. A deep-blue body with red seats and red trimmings was a favorite color scheme. If the countryman liked touches of originality, it was always acceptable to have a border of flowers, or even a motto, on the dashboard. A color combination of emphasis, a new buggy whip, a warm buffalo robe, and a horse with zip and life—then a lad thoroughly enjoyed a pung ride to town on a sunny day in midwinter.

Hauling Out the Wood

W HEN WINTER HAS TURNED THE CORNER INTO FEBRU-
ary and the piles of gray birch, maple, and oak are
dotted around the wood lot, comes the time to haul out the
wood. During the gray days of December and January a
farmer likes to get the chopping done. Then, after the January thaw and before one of the big snows of ground-hog time,
there is usually a period of good sledding.

Many a farm lad who sees little glamour in splitting wood
and less in stacking it in the woodshed, enjoys a Saturday's
work in hauling it from the wood lot. A one-horse bob with
its four tall, sturdy oak stakes is a good vehicle to handle.
Belle, the Morgan mare, insists on trotting across the mowing
field, up the grade of the sidehill pasture, and along the road
that winds through the maple-sugar grove and into the wood
lot.

Loading the wood upon the sled is satisfying work. There's
no particular sense of urgency, as in haying or in digging potatoes. If a chap wants to follow a rabbit's track a spell, that
is part of the day's routine. Possibly there may be a partridge
lurking in that thicket. Here's where the red fox trotted
slowly by early in the morning. The blue jays flash among the
trees, shouting raucously that the sun is climbing higher and
spring's around the corner. An insistent chickadee calls for
attention as he does acrobatic feats around the tree limbs.

The bobsled, piled high, slides smoothly down to the yard
behind the woodshed. On a snappy, still day the steel runners
squeak on the snow, and the horse's shoes make a crunchy,
edgy sound as the iron bites into the packed-down sled track.
Hauling out the wood for next season's supply is satisfying
labor. Stoves, furnaces, and fireplaces use a big amount.
Many a man who has fought his way upward in our demo-
cratic society can remember the time in winter when it was
his share of the family work to haul out the wood.

F. W. Wenn

COLD HAS SEALED THE PONDS, LAKES, AND RIVERS; AND across the Northern states farmers are getting up the ice. In the fall, before freezing weather set in, the old weather-beaten icehouse was cleaned of its damp, pungent sawdust—except a few inches at the bottom.

It's a colorful, picturesque sight on the village pond, these winter days, reminiscent of a Currier & Ives country scene. Men and boys are pulling the long, big-toothed ice saws up and down, cutting the rectangular blocks that have previously been marked out by the horse-drawn ice plow. Others are pushing lines of blocks through the dark, crackling water to the edge of the pond. Here the blocks are pulled from the water and loaded upon the farmers' trucks. A good, snappy day is best for harvesting ice. Then the cakes dry quickly when taken from the water.

At the farm, the blocks are pushed up a smooth oak or maple plank into the icehouse. Building a pile of ice isn't so ticklish as building a load of hay, but it has to be done correctly or there'll be trouble next summer. A thin scattering of sawdust between layers prevents the cakes from sticking too closely to each other. If the blocks have a quarter-inch space between them in the layer, a farm boy can get them out more easily. Getting up the ice is good work. It's work a boy enjoys on a Saturday. Ice not only goes into the milk tank and the refrigerator, it will help to make a gallon freezer of ice cream on a hot day next summer.

*W*HEN THE R.F.D. MAN HANDS OVER THE FAMILIAR, paper-covered book, it means that spring is coming, that winter will surely end.

There are differing philosophies regarding seed catalogues. Some peruse them as factual documents and can take the adjectives and pictures in stride. Others affect a tolerant skepticism. Seed catalogues, they imply, are an accepted part of the great business of publishing words and pictures. They regard the photographs and drawings with a mild degree of interest; but, as is the case in many conclaves and conferences, they have reservations.

The countryman, however, belongs to a third and larger group. He makes no mental reservations. To him the seed catalogues are a valued part of the year's reading. They are as natural a part of January on the farm as are the mail-order catalogues in March and September. From long experience he knows how to read the seed catalogues in comfortable relaxation. After the chores are done and his heavy boots are stalled behind the kitchen stove, he pulls up the old Morris chair, adjusts the flame of the lamp on the end of the table, puts his feet in the oven, and settles down to a couple of hours of solid enjoyment.

What does it matter if the beautifully symmetrical gardens displayed never show a weed? That's a goal for good husbandmen. Why get unduly excited over mammoth tomatoes, militarily exact rows of sweet corn, each stalk with three or four ears? And that gorgeous painting of a field thickly dotted with big, plump golden squashes! The adjectives may follow each other in mounting ecstasy, but it's all part of a good solid tradition. The important thing is that it's seed-catalogue time. Neither wars nor rumors of wars can stop that. If seed catalogues were omitted from our annual publishing output, it would leave an uneasy void in our winter's literature.